Women Who Dare

Catalog No. 97114
Published by Pomegranate Calendars & Books, Box 6099, Rohnert Park, California 94927
© 1996 Library of Congress

Available in Canada from Firefly Books Ltd.,
250 Sparks Avenue, Willowdale, Ontario M2H 2S4
Available in the U.K. and mainland Europe from Pomegranate Europe Ltd.,
Fullbridge House, Fullbridge, Maldon, Essex CM9 7LE, England
Available in Australia from Boobook Publications Pty. Ltd.,
P.O. Box 163 or Freepost 1, Tea Gardens 2324
Available in New Zealand from Randy Horwood Ltd.,
P.O. Box 32-077, Devonport, Auckland
Available in Asia (including the Middle East), Africa, and Latin America from
Pomegranate Pacific Ltd., 113 Babcombe Drive, Thornhill, Ontario L3T 1M9, Canada

Pomegranate publishes many calendars on a variety of subjects, from fine art and architecture to literature, music, and the environment. Our catalog showing over 150 1997 calendars is available for one dollar. We also offer other full-color catalogs (illustrating our notecards, holiday cards, boxed notes, gift enclosures, postcards, books of postcards, blank books, address books, books of days, posters, art magnets, knowledge cards, bookmarks, journals, and books) for nominal fees.
For more information on obtaining catalogs and ordering, please write to
Pomegranate, Box 6099, Rohnert Park, California 94927.

Cover design by Young Jin Kim

ISBN 0-87654-717-X $12.95
53 color reproductions   112 pages   Available August 1, 1996

LIBRARY OF CONGRESS 1997 ENGAGEMENT CALENDAR

Welcome to the fourth edition of *Women Who Dare*, featuring stories and images from the incomparable collections of the Library of Congress.

Herein are artists, activists, businesswomen, scientists, quiet dreamers, revolutionaries. Each one, in struggling to realize her own vision in her particular circumstances, has made a unique contribution to the world—and to a unique store of human inspiration, so long hidden from view, whose legacy can as yet only be imagined.

Compiler and editor: Susan Sharp
Writers: Susan Sharp, Lynne Shaner, Margaret Wagner
Researchers: Athena Angelos, Christine Hauser
Photographs: Library of Congress collections, except as noted
Additional photography: Jim Higgins, Yusef El-Amin

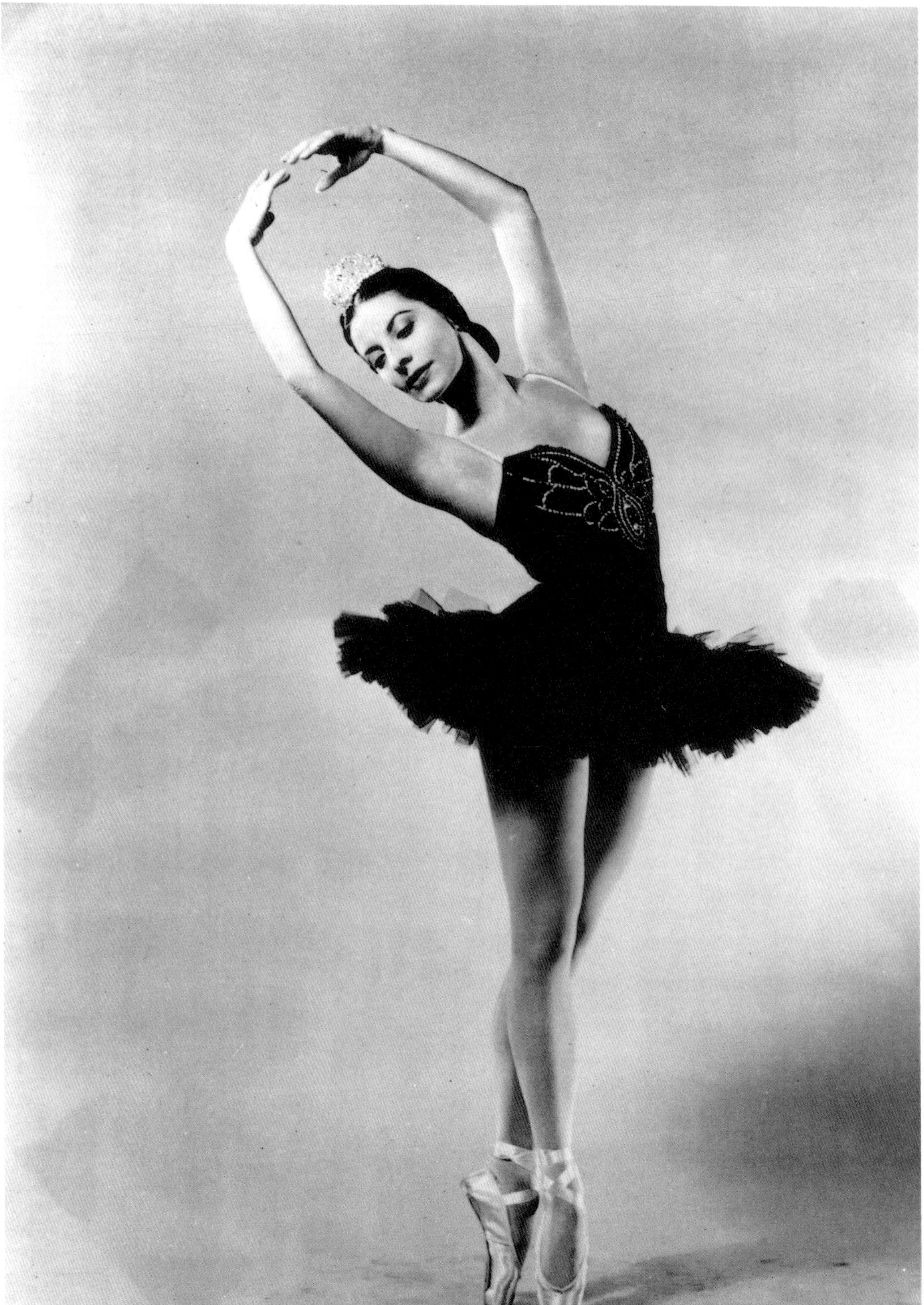

Dec/Jan

JANUARY
S	M	T	W	T	F	S
			1	2	3	4
5	6	7	8	9	10	11
12	13	14	15	16	17	18
19	20	21	22	23	24	25
26	27	28	29	30	31	

ALICIA ALONSO
(b. 1921)
Dancer, choreographer

A veritable one-person cultural force, Alicia Alonso has distinguished herself not only as one of the great ballerinas of the century but also as an amazing example of the power of a single artist to inspire and create opportunity for others.

Born in Havana, Alonso was drawn to dance early. After training formally in Cuba, she studied with Muriel Stuart and George Balanchine in New York City and was soon dancing with the American Ballet Theatre. Her technical brilliance and riveting stage presence had brought her to the brink of fame at age nineteen when a detached retina temporarily blinded her and necessitated a series of harrowing operations that immobilized her for more than a year. Dauntless, Alonso founded her own company in Cuba in 1948. As others fled Cuba, she returned permanently, reconstituting her company as the Ballet Nacional de Cuba, building it into a world-class ensemble, and promoting arts education, appreciation, and involvement at every level of society.

New York World-Telegram and Sun Collection
Prints and Photographs Division

365
Rachel Foster Avery, suffragist and assistant to Susan B. Anthony, b. 1858

30
Monday

366
Singer and songwriter Odetta b. 1930

31
Tuesday

1
Betsy Ross b. 1752

1
New Year's Day
Wednesday

2
M. Carey Thomas, pioneer of women's higher education, b. 1857

2
Last Quarter
Thursday

3
Lucretia Coffin Mott, abolitionist and women's rights leader, b. 1793

3
Friday

4
Selena Butler, advocate-leader of interracial cooperation, b. 1872

4
Saturday

5
Olympia Brown, pacifist and Universalist minister, b. 1835

5
Sunday

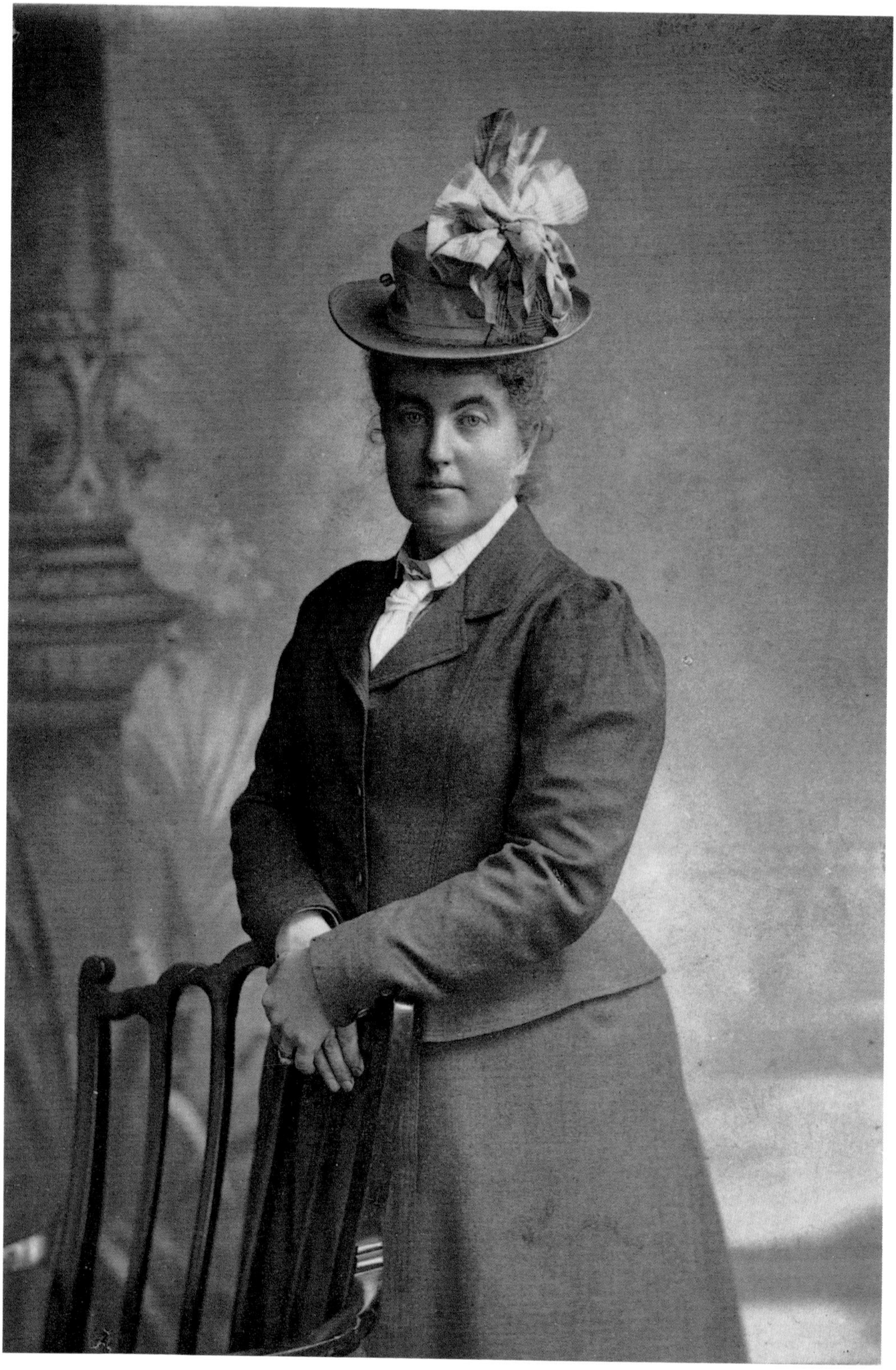

January

S	M	T	W	T	F	S
			1	2	3	4
5	6	7	8	9	10	11
12	13	14	15	16	17	18
19	20	21	22	23	24	25
26	27	28	29	30	31	

FANNY BULLOCK WORKMAN
(1859–1925)
Adventurer, author

"Barcelona," wrote Fanny Bullock Workman, "is not a pleasant place for a woman to visit with a bicycle. . . . Even in a regulation street gown she cannot walk a block alone without being rudely spoken to." While Workman made note of such annoyances, they hardly stopped her during the bicycle tours she made with her husband through Algeria and Spain in 1895. The couple wrote two books about the experience before going on to India and then to the Himalayas, where they would make a total of eight expeditions into the then-unexplored Karakoram range, making significant contributions to geographical and anthropological knowledge. *In the Ice World of Himalaya* (1905) was the first of their five books describing the fantastic Himalayan terrain.

Among the records in which Workman took pride was being the first female mountaineer to reach an altitude over 23,000 feet (1906). Unlike other world-class climbers, Workman accomplished most of her treks in the long skirts that were *de rigueur* for a lady of the time.

Prints and Photographs Division

Joan of Arc b. 1412

6 Monday

Marian Anderson debuts at the Metropolitan Opera, 1955

7 Tuesday

Fanny Bullock Workman, pioneering travel writer, b. 1859

8 Wednesday

Carrie Chapman Catt, engineer of "winning plan" that gained passage of the 19th Amendment (woman suffrage), b. 1859

New Moon

9 Thursday

Katharine Burr Blodgett, developer of the first nonreflecting glass, b. 1898

10 Friday

Amelia Earhart leaves Honolulu on first solo flight across the Pacific, 1935

11 Saturday

Playwright Lorraine Hansberry d. 1901

12 Sunday

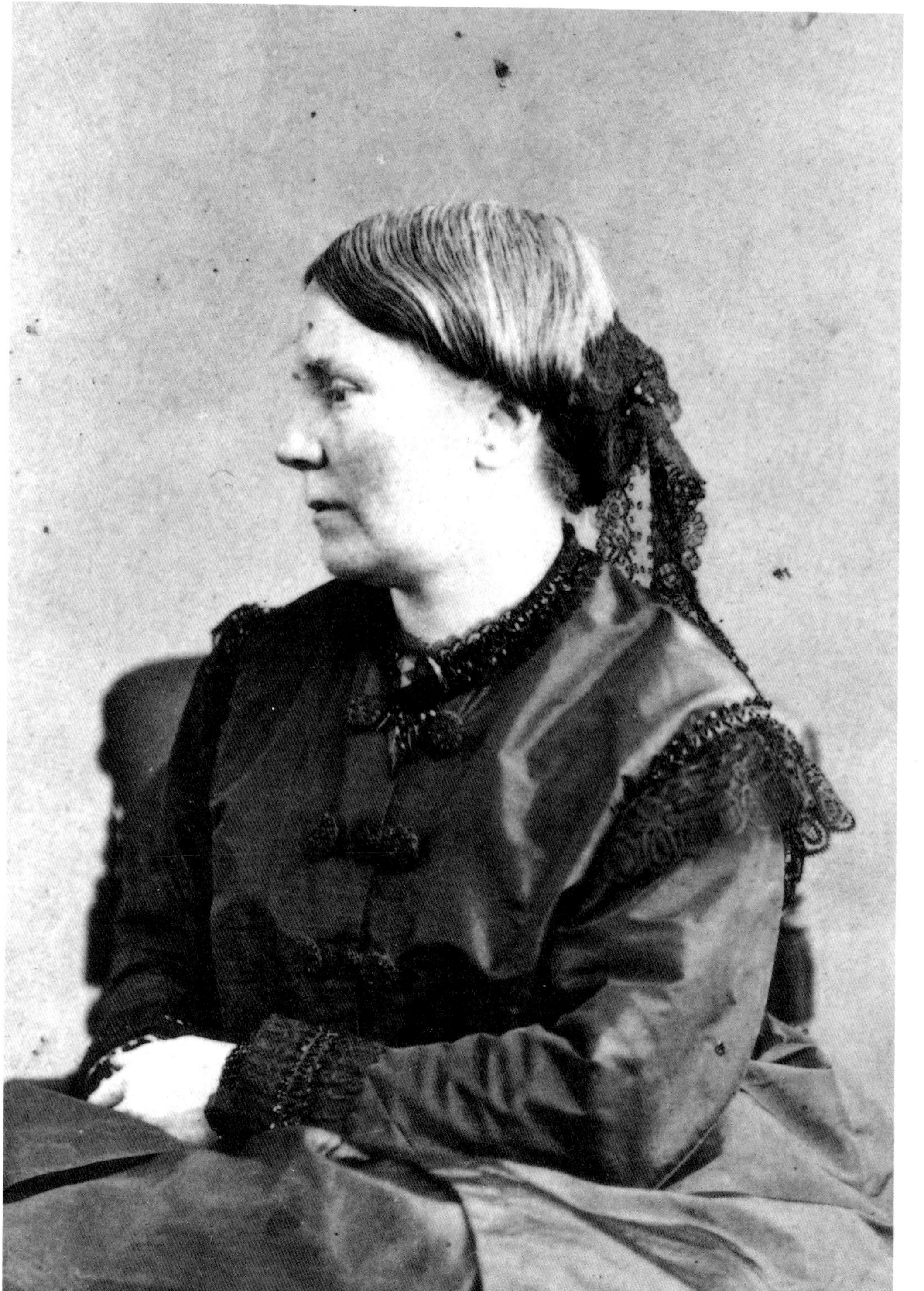

January

S	M	T	W	T	F	S
			1	2	3	4
5	6	7	8	9	10	11
12	13	14	15	16	17	18
19	20	21	22	23	24	25
26	27	28	29	30	31	

ELIZABETH BLACKWELL
(1821–1910)
Physician

A pioneer for women's health and women's rights, Elizabeth Blackwell became the first modern woman to break through the centuries-old exclusion of women from the practice of medicine. Educated by tutors as a girl, Blackwell first studied medicine on her own. Then, wishing to practice formally, she applied to many U.S. medical schools. All rejected her because of gender prejudice until, at last, she was admitted to Geneva Medical College in New York, from which she received her degree in 1849. After completing her internship in her native England, she returned to the United States—to find no hospital willing to hire female physicians. So, with her sister Emily and Marie Zackrzewska, both of whom had also achieved medical degrees, Blackwell opened a clinic in the slums of New York City. The clinic's success led to the three women's opening the New York Infirmary for Women and Children, to which they later attached a medical college for women, the first of its kind. Blackwell continued her promotion of women in medicine for many years via her activities in the medical community and through her writings.

Manuscript Division

Charlotte Ray, first black female lawyer in the U.S., b. 1850

13
Monday

The Massachusetts colony holds a day of fasting to take "the blame and the shame" for the Salem witch trials and executions, 1697

14
Tuesday

Jeannette Rankin, age 87, leads 5,000 women in a march on Capitol Hill protesting the Vietnam War, 1968

Martin Luther King Jr.'s Birthday
First Quarter

15
Wednesday

Writer and thinker Susan Sontag b. 1933

16
Thursday

Martha Cotera, Chicana feminist, librarian, and civil rights worker, b. 1938

17
Friday

Alice Putnam, kindergarten advocate in the 1870s, b. 1841

18
Saturday

Janis Joplin b. 1943

19
Sunday

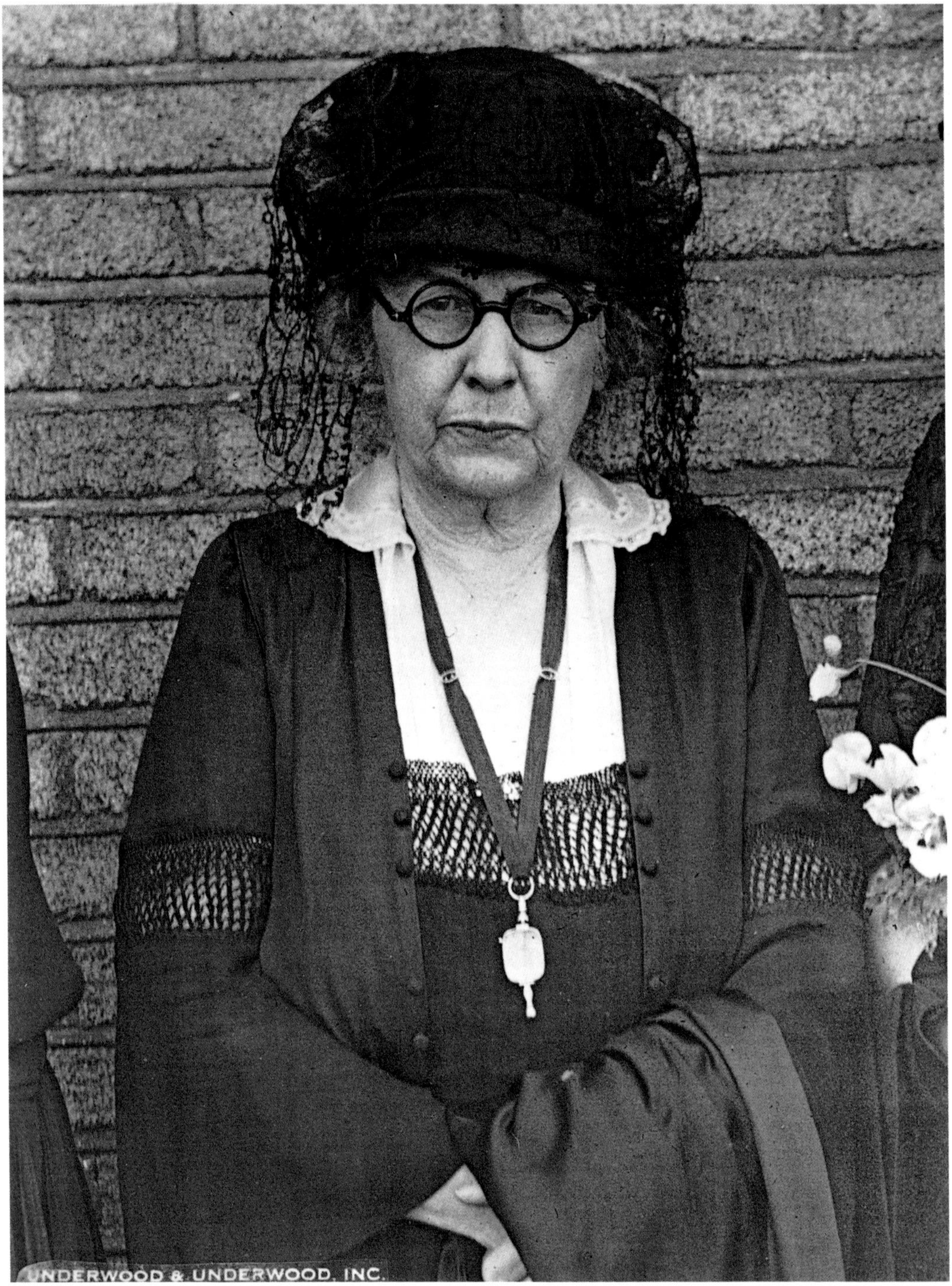
UNDERWOOD & UNDERWOOD, INC.

January

S	M	T	W	T	F	S
			1	2	3	4
5	6	7	8	9	10	11
12	13	14	15	16	17	18
19	20	21	22	23	24	25
26	27	28	29	30	31	

HARRIOT STANTON BLATCH
(1856–1940)
Suffragist, political leader

It was Sojourner [Truth] who first gave my pride in my glib reading ability a decided jolt. The duty was assigned to me to read the morning papers to Sojourner as she sat smoking her pipe. One morning, greatly puzzled, I ventured the question . . . "Sojourner, can't you read?" "Oh no, honey," she answered quickly, "I can't read little things like letters. I read big things like men."

—H. S. Blatch, *Challenging Years* (1940)

Harriot Stanton Blatch grew up amid many of the icons of the movement for women's rights, and those such as Sojourner Truth helped extend her vision to issues of class and race. Daughter of Elizabeth Cady Stanton, Blatch was a feminist activist at Vassar, and when marriage took her to England, she lent her efforts to the suffrage movement there. After her return in 1902 she became a key figure in revitalizing the U.S. suffrage movement, founding the League of Self-Supporting Women. She also advocated pay for women's work in the home. This photograph was taken during her 1921 campaign for Comptroller of the City of New York.

Prints and Photographs Division

---

20 Monday
Harriot Stanton Blatch, suffragist and political activist, b. 1856

Martin Luther King Jr.'s Birthday (Observed)

21 Tuesday
Sophia Louisa Jex-Blake, English physician who secured the rights of her countrywomen to study and practice medicine, b. 1840

22 Wednesday
Elaine Noble, Massachusetts state legislator and lesbian rights activist, b. 1944

23 Thursday
Elizabeth Blackwell becomes the first woman in the U.S. to gain an M.D. degree, 1849

Full Moon

24 Friday
Dr. Mary Edwards Walker receives the Medal of Honor for her Civil War service, 1866

25 Saturday
Clarina Nichols, Kansas lecturer on suffrage and abolitionism, b. 1810

26 Sunday
Wu Yi Fang, first and only female college president in China before communism, b. 1893

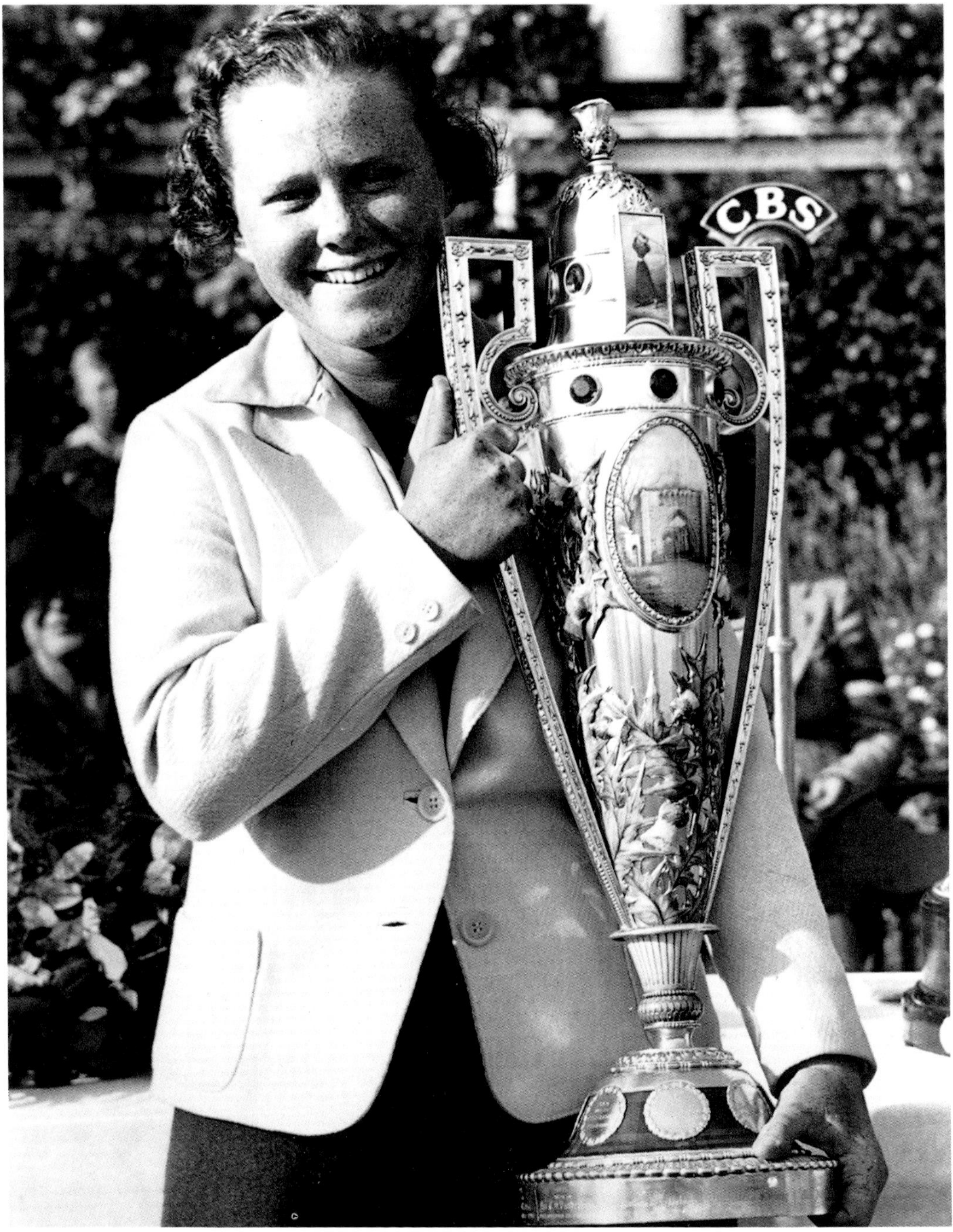
CBS

Jan/Feb

FEBRUARY
S	M	T	W	T	F	S
						1
2	3	4	5	6	7	8
9	10	11	12	13	14	15
16	17	18	19	20	21	22
23	24	25	26	27	28	

PATTY BERG
(b. 1918)
Golfer

An early starter on the path to becoming an outstanding sportswoman—she quarterbacked her hometown street football team, played sandlot baseball, skated in the junior speed skating championships, and ran for the track team—Patty Berg went on to an unprecedented career in golf and became one of the legends of the game. After winning twenty-nine amateur titles, she turned pro in 1940, a time when there were only three tournaments—with low prize money—for professional female golfers. With Babe Didrikson Zaharias, Berg founded the Ladies Professional Golf Association (LPGA) and served as its first president. She went on to win more than fifty-seven professional titles, including forty-one LPGA titles, and was the first woman to reach $100,000 in career earnings. Throughout her career, Berg also worked to expand the game for women. Her many honors include membership in the International Women's Sports Hall of Fame.

New York World-Telegram and Sun Collection
Prints and Photographs Division

27
Gospel legend Mahalia Jackson dies in Evergreen Park, Ill., 1972

27
Monday

28
Author Colette b. 1873

28
Tuesday

29
Violette Neatley Anderson, first African American woman to practice before the U.S. Supreme Court, b. 1926

29
Wednesday

30
Sharon Pratt Kelly, first female mayor of the District of Columbia, b. 1944

30
Thursday

31
Entertainer Carol Channing b. 1923

Last Quarter

31
Friday

32
First U.S. postage stamp to honor an African American woman (Harriet Tubman) is issued, 1978

1
Saturday

33
Physician Sara Stevenson, first female member of the American Medical Association, b. 1841

2
Sunday

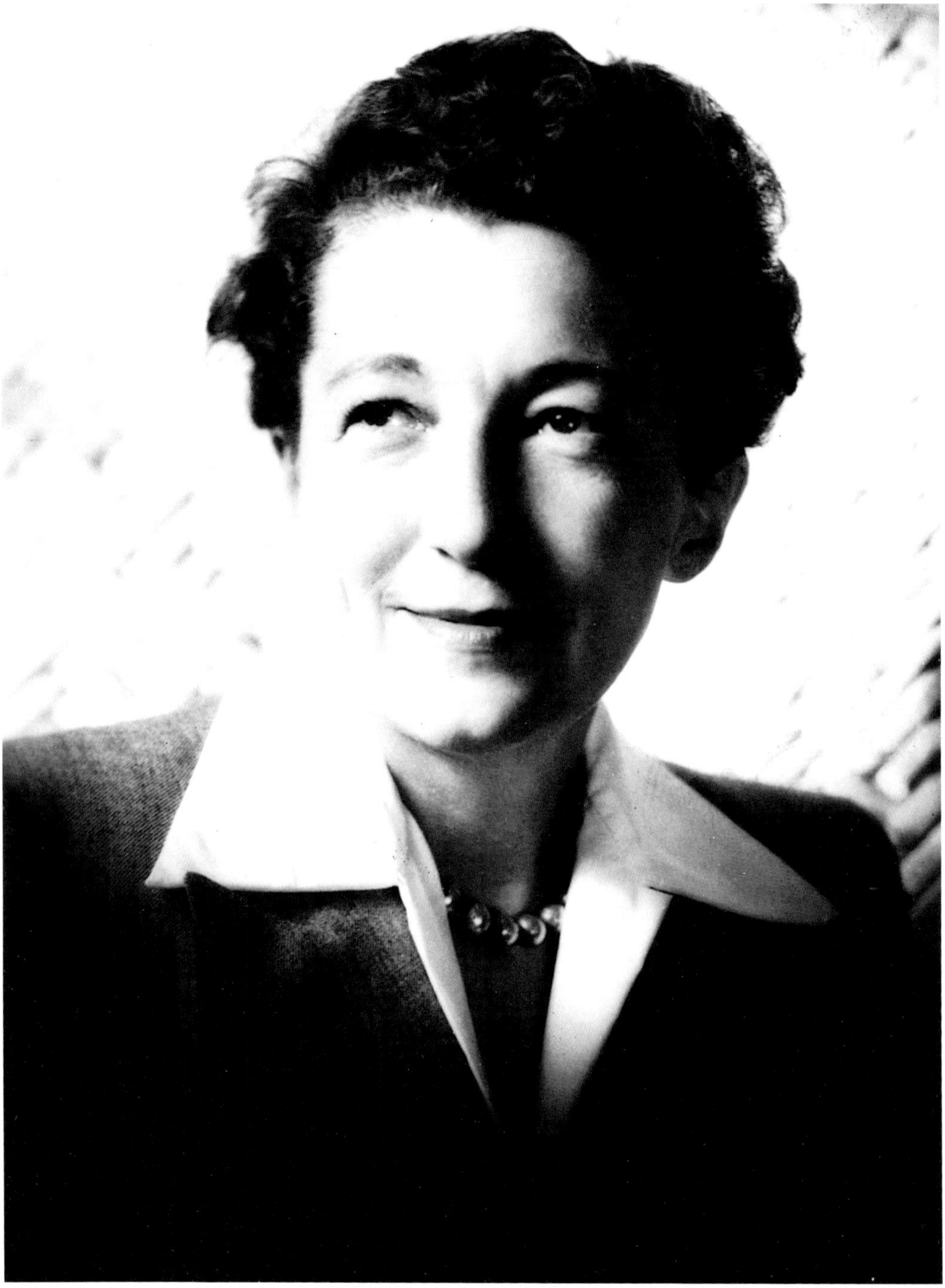

February

S	M	T	W	T	F	S
						1
2	3	4	5	6	7	8
9	10	11	12	13	14	15
16	17	18	19	20	21	22
23	24	25	26	27	28	

MILDRED CAPRON
(1899–1978)
Filmmaker, lecturer

The Society of Woman Geographers (SWG), in an annual questionnaire, asked its members to fill in their "special interest within the geographical field." Mildred Capron's answer, in 1962: "Interpreting a relatively small area through the film-medium; historic background; essentials of the business of living; folk arts and industries; PEOPLE, at work and at play." Among the geographic areas Capron documented and interpreted were Ireland, South Africa, Portugal, Alaska, Brittany, the Azores, and Chesapeake Bay. In short, Capron spent her life traveling and filming the world and making a living at it. A promotional brochure for Capron Films includes this terse bio: "An Easterner by birth, she lived in China for 14 years and has been twice around the globe. Now she calls Wyoming 'home.'" Capron usually summered with fellow SWG member Mardy Murie at a ranch in Moose, Wyoming, where she eventually retired. Two years before she died she reported to the Society: "Busy as a bird dog."

Society of Woman Geographers Collection
Manuscript Division

Pioneering physician Elizabeth Blackwell b. 1821

3 Monday — 34

Mildred Capron, documentary filmmaker, b. 1899

4 Tuesday — 35

Mary Gardner, who professionalized public health nursing in the U.S. and Europe, b. 1871

5 Wednesday — 36

Pauline Agassiz Shaw, kindergarten and day-care pioneer, b. 1841

6 Thursday — 37

Swiss women gain the right to vote, 1971

New Moon

7 Friday — 38

Elizabeth II is proclaimed queen of England, 1952

8 Saturday — 39

Poet Amy Lowell b. 1874

9 Sunday — 40

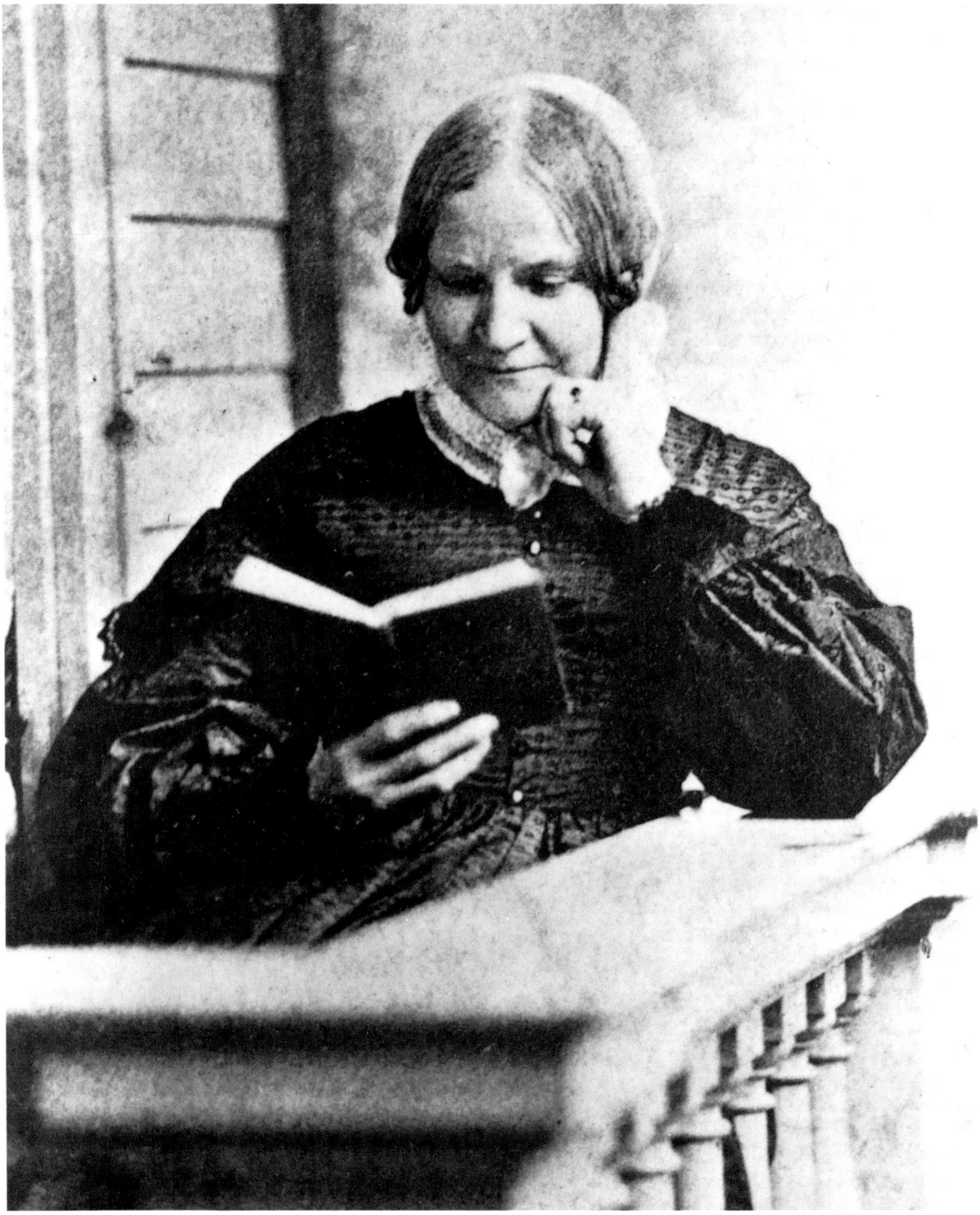

February

S	M	T	W	T	F	S
						1
2	3	4	5	6	7	8
9	10	11	12	13	14	15
16	17	18	19	20	21	22
23	24	25	26	27	28	

LYDIA MARIA CHILD
(1802–1880)
Abolitionist, author

A major literary figure of her time, Lydia Maria Child was first exposed to the progressive thought and literature of the day through her brother, a Unitarian minister whose frequent guests included Whittier and Emerson. At age twenty-two she first gained attention with the novel *Hobomok,* based on the Abenaki Indian lore she had grown up with. Other novels and magazine pieces followed, and after her 1928 marriage to abolitionist lawyer David Child, she expanded her scope to include domestic feminism and home management. The influential *Frugal Housewife* (1830) was a forerunner of the domestic manuals that would bring fame to Catherine Beecher and Sara Josepha Hale. Child's antislavery sentiments were first given powerful voice in *An Appeal in Favor of That Class of Americans Called Africans* (1833); it cost her dearly in popularity, but she continued to write on that and many other subjects. The year 1841, for example, found her living in New York and editing the *Anti-Slavery Standard,* lodging at a Quaker home that doubled as a "station" on the underground railroad.

Prints and Photographs Division

41
Pioneering electrical engineer Edith Clarke b. 1883

10
Monday

42
Lydia Maria Child, author of influential antislavery works and volumes of advice for women, b. 1802

11
Tuesday

43
Juliette Gordon Low establishes the Girl Guides, forerunner of the Girl Scouts of America, 1912

Lincoln's Birthday
Ash Wednesday

12
Wednesday

44
Champion golfer Patty Berg b. 1918

13
Thursday

45
Inventor Margaret E. Knight, who held 27 patents and was called the "female Edison," b. 1838

Valentine's Day
First Quarter

14
Friday

46
Author Susan Brownmiller b. 1935

15
Saturday

47
First women's six-day bicycle race ends at Madison Square Garden, New York City, 1889

16
Sunday

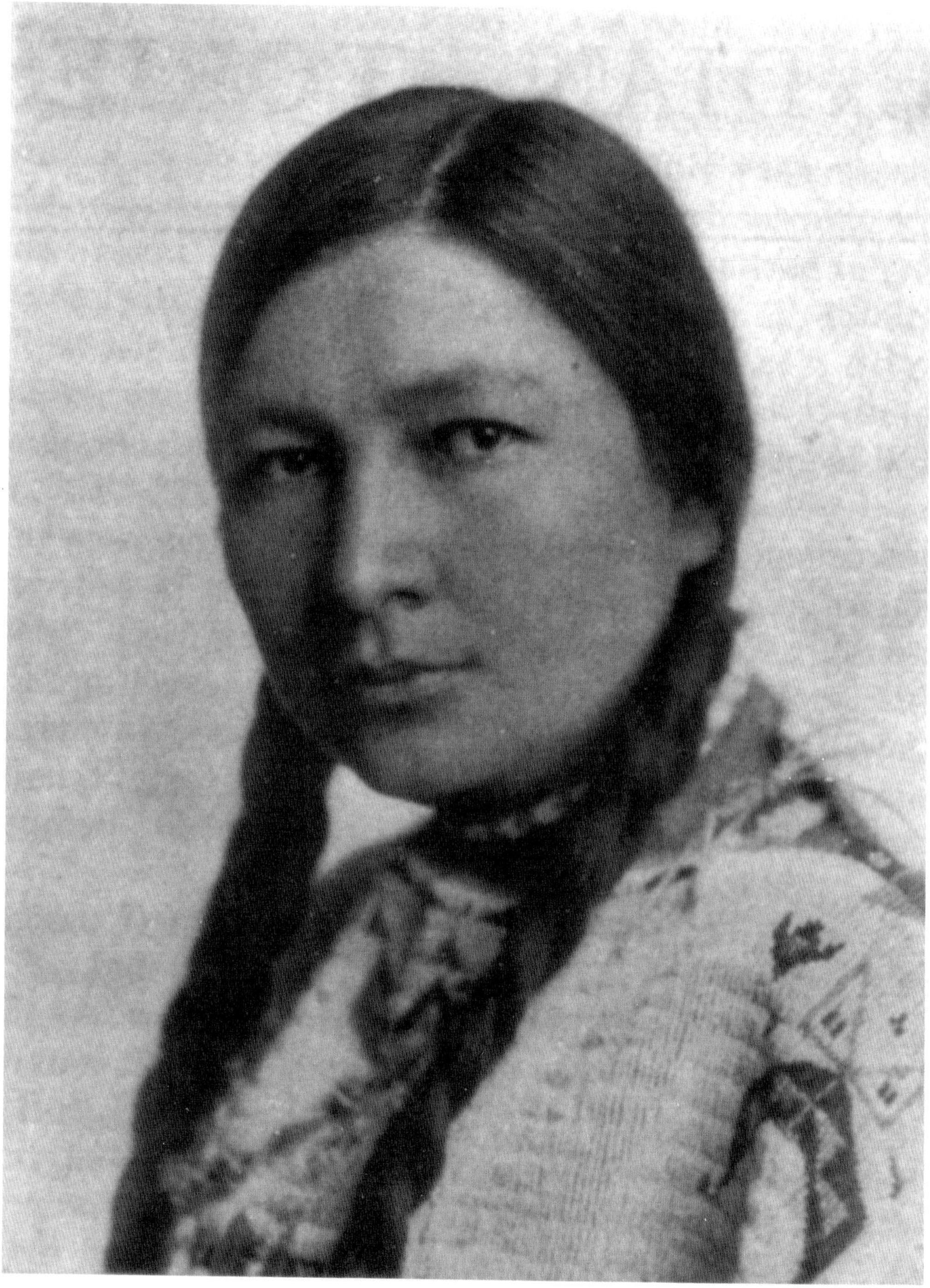

February

S	M	T	W	T	F	S
						1
2	3	4	5	6	7	8
9	10	11	12	13	14	15
16	17	18	19	20	21	22
23	24	25	26	27	28	

GERTRUDE SIMMONS BONNIN (ZITKALA-SA)
(1876–1938)
Writer, activist

"While the old people last, I want to get from them their treasured ideas of life," Gertrude Simmons Bonnin once said. Bonnin, who renamed herself Zitkala-Sa, or "Red Bird," became one of the first Native Americans to translate and publish the stories she had grown up with, depicting Indian lifestyles in a variety of publications. Her first book, *Old Indian Legends,* was a collection of Sioux tales, and *American Indian Stories* comprised autobiographical essays about being a Native American. A Yankton Sioux, Bonnin was born at a time when Native Americans were not legally American citizens, when government policy was to separate Indian children from their homes for as long as possible, to indoctrinate them into white culture. Taught to read and write in English, Bonnin seemed caught between the white world and that of Indians. Independent, she established a place for herself; loyal to her cultural heritage, she devoted her life to speaking out on behalf of other American Indians.
General Collections

Julia De Burgos, Puerto Rican poet and journalist, b. 1914

Presidents' Day

48
17
Monday

Author and Nobel laureate Toni Morrison b. 1931

49
18
Tuesday

Short-story writer and novelist Kay Boyle b. 1902

50
19
Wednesday

Gloria Vanderbilt, fashion mogul, artist, and actor, b. 1924

51
20
Thursday

Barbara Jordan, first congresswoman from the Deep South, b. 1936

52
21
Friday

Sioux activist Gertrude Simmons Bonnin b. 1876

Washington's Birthday
Full Moon

53
22
Saturday

Fannie Merritt Farmer, author who standardized cooking measurements, b. 1857

54
23
Sunday

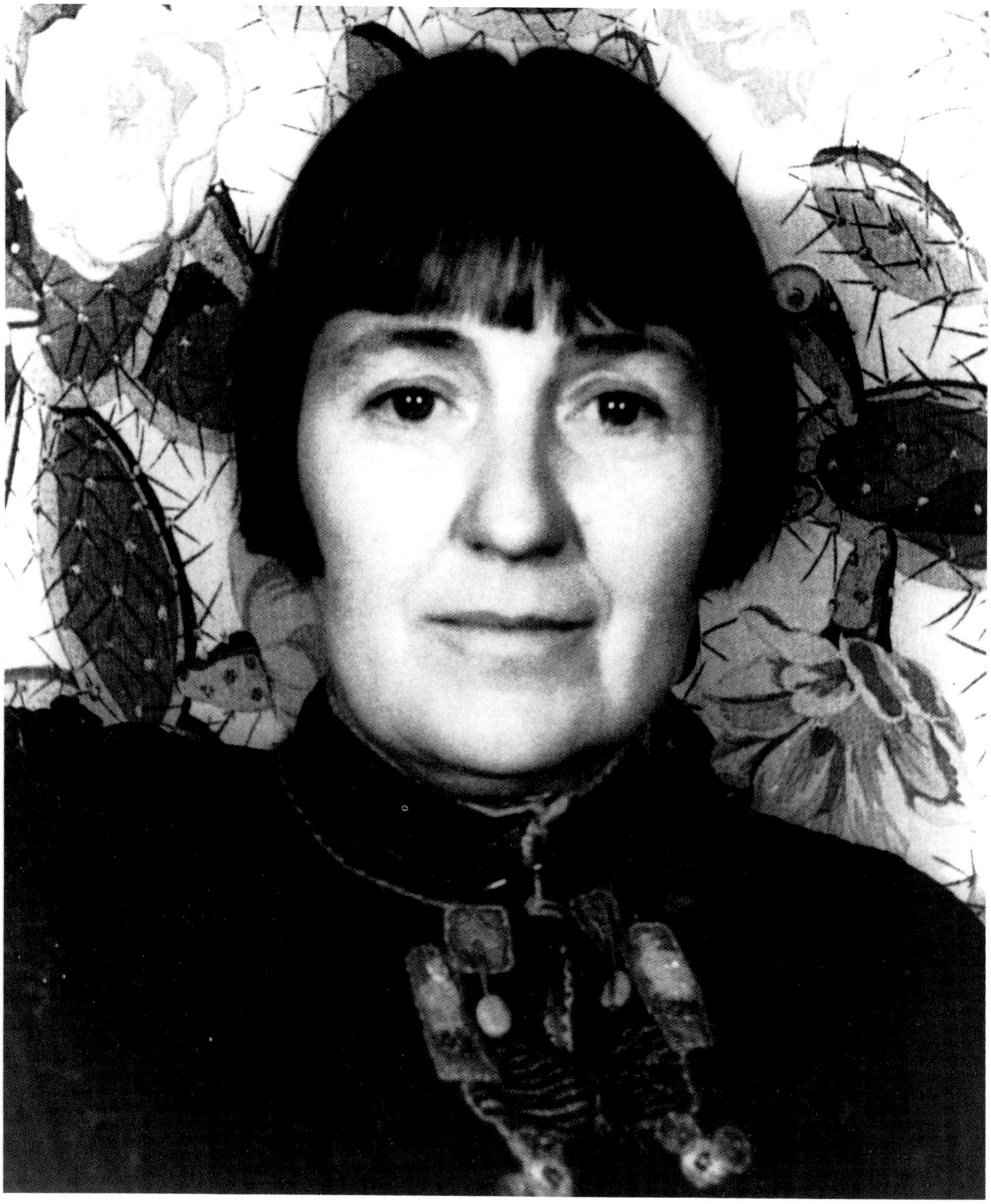

Feb/Mar

MARCH

S	M	T	W	T	F	S
						1
2	3	4	5	6	7	8
9	10	11	12	13	14	15
16	17	18	19	20	21	22
23	24	25	26	27	28	29
30	31					

MABEL DODGE LUHAN
(1879–1962)
Writer, salonniere

Mabel Dodge Luhan collected people and revealed them—and herself—in her four-volume *Intimate Memories* and other autobiographical works. Born into wealth, she traveled widely, married severally, and interfered remarkably (for good *and* ill) in the lives of an imposing array of friends. Leo and Gertrude Stein, Carl Van Vechten, Isadora Duncan, Walter Lippmann, Emma Goldman, Robinson Jeffers, Edwin Arlington Robinson, John Reed (with whom she had an intense love affair), and D. H. and Frieda Lawrence were among the movers and shakers who attended her literary salons and otherwise populated her privileged world. After the death of her first husband, she married architect Edwin Dodge and lived with him in Italy. New York City was home during her third marriage, to artist Maurice Stern. Finally, she settled in Taos, New Mexico, gathering place for artists and writers, home of her fourth husband, Pueblo Indian Tony Luhan, and the setting for four of her books.

Photograph by Carl Van Vechten
Prints and Photographs Division

Author and educator Mary Ellen Chase b. 1887
24 Monday — 55

Nutrition writer Adelle Davis b. 1904
25 Tuesday — 56

Memoirist Mabel Dodge Luhan b. 1879
26 Wednesday — 57

Actor and AIDS activist Elizabeth Taylor b. 1932
27 Thursday — 58

Actor and singer Bernadette Peters b. 1948
28 Friday — 59

Rebecca Lee of Boston, Mass., becomes the first African American woman to gain a medical degree, 1864
1 Saturday — 60

Last Quarter

Women begin pilot training for the U.S. Navy, 1973
2 Sunday — 61

Calamity Jane, Gen. Crook's Scout.
Copyrighted by H. R. Locke, 1895.

March

S	M	T	W	T	F	S
						1
2	3	4	5	6	7	8
9	10	11	12	13	14	15
16	17	18	19	20	21	22
23	24	25	26	27	28	29
30	31					

CALAMITY JANE (MARTHA JANE CANNARY)
(1852?–1903)
Frontierswoman

Born in Missouri and raised in Montana, Martha Jane Cannary grew up to become a sharpshooting, hard-riding, gender nonconformist of the Old West whose colorful life has become part of its folklore.

Though accounts of her life are sketchy, Cannary appears to have lost both parents at about age twelve, after which she became a drifter in the mining districts of Montana. An excellent markswoman and rider from an early age, she also developed a fondness for liquor and, not surprisingly, a distaste for wearing women's clothing. In the 1870s she served as a scout for various military and geological expeditions, eventually settling for a time in Deadwood, South Dakota, during its gold-mining heyday. Her lovers included Wild Bill Hickock, and her occupations ran a gamut from mail carrier to sometime prostitute.

The nickname "Calamity Jane" was probably derived either from the compassion she showed the unfortunate (as in her assisting the sick in the smallpox epidemic of 1878) or from the warning she gave men who might get on her wrong side.

Prints and Photographs Division

Track star and Olympic medalist Jackie Joyner-Kersee b. 1962

3
Monday

Jeannette Rankin of Montana is sworn in as the first female member of Congress, 1917

4
Tuesday

Lady Isabella Gregory, Irish playwright and founder of the Abbey Theatre, b. 1852

5
Wednesday

Eleanor Roosevelt becomes the first First Lady to travel by air to a foreign country, 1934

6
Thursday

Singer Billie Holiday b. 1915

7
Friday

Jockey Barbara Jo Rubin b. 1969

8
Saturday

English actor Glenda Jackson b. 1936

New Moon

9
Sunday

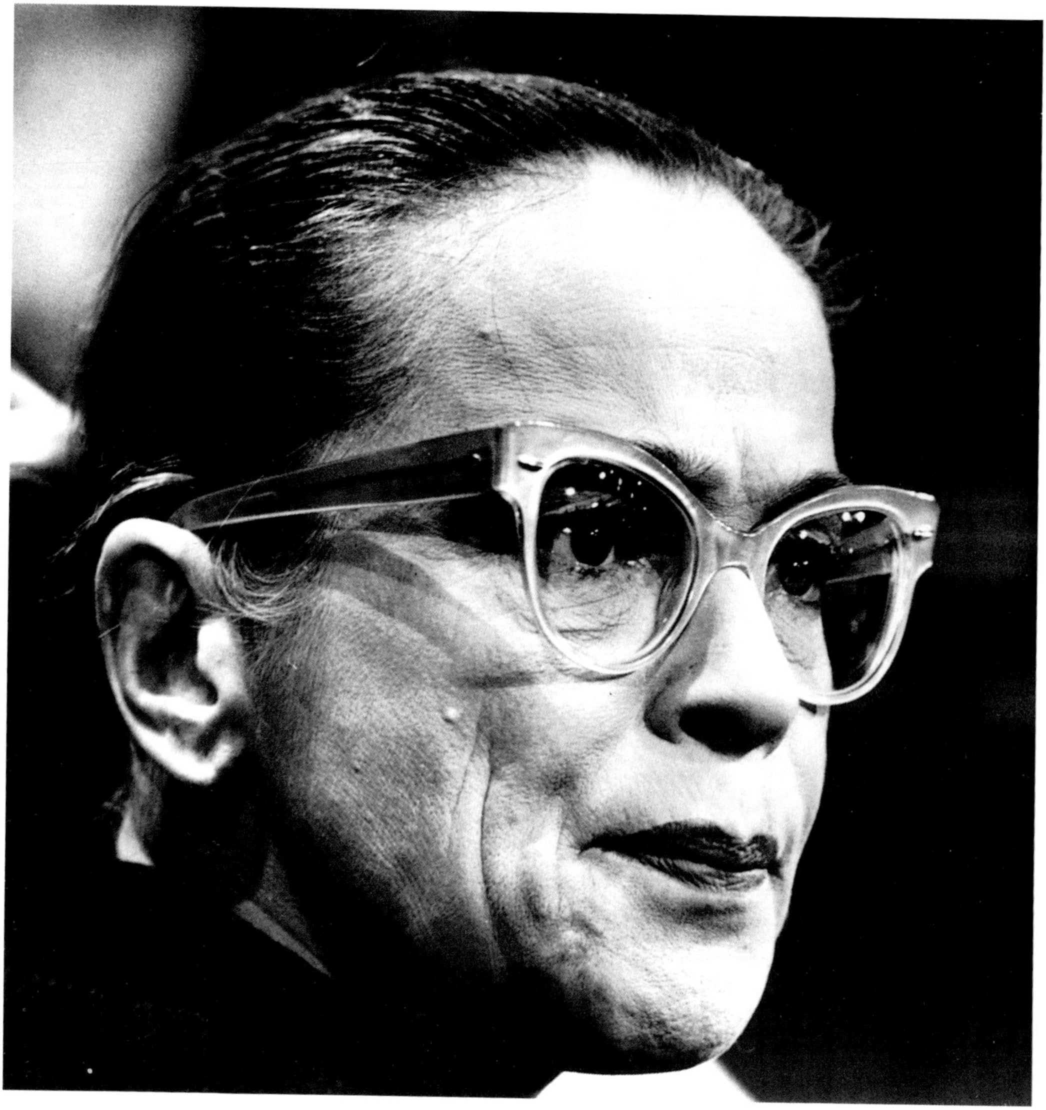

March

S	M	T	W	T	F	S
						1
2	3	4	5	6	7	8
9	10	11	12	13	14	15
16	17	18	19	20	21	22
23	24	25	26	27	28	29
30	31					

DICKEY CHAPPELLE
(1918–1965)
Photojournalist,
war correspondent

Born Georgette Meyer in Milwaukee, Wisconsin, Dickey Chappelle became one of the few women to penetrate the top ranks of combat correspondents during World War II and the Vietnam War. Fascinated with aviation and brilliant at math, she entered MIT on a full scholarship at age sixteen. After learning to fly and skydive, she worked for a time as a parachutist in air shows before taking up photography and becoming an accredited correspondent.

Her assignments during World War II included Iwo Jima and Okinawa in the Pacific, and she went on to report on Hungary, Algeria, Cuba, and finally Vietnam, where she made more than thirty parachute jumps before becoming the first female correspondent to die in that war. Chappelle's reports revealed the human toll of the wars she covered, one reason she was regarded with particular affection by the servicemen she was covering. The year she died, the 82nd Airborne Division named a parachute drop zone in her honor.

New York World-Telegram and Sun Collection
Prints and Photographs Division

Women's rights activist Hallie Quinn Brown b. 1845

10 Monday — 69

Mme. d'Epinay, author who won fame with her *Conversations of Emily* and *Memoirs and Correspondence*, b. 1726

11 Tuesday — 70

Annette Adams, first female federal prosecutor, b. 1877

12 Wednesday — 71

Susan B. Anthony dies at age 86, leaving her $10,000 estate to the cause of woman suffrage, 1906

13 Thursday — 72

Lucy Hobbs Taylor, first woman to obtain a dental degree in the U.S., b. 1833

14 Friday — 73

Margaret Webster, first female director at the Metropolitan Opera House in New York City, b. 1905

15 Saturday — 74

Aviator Margie Hurley becomes the first woman to break the 300 m.p.h. airspeed barrier, 1947

First Quarter

16 Sunday — 75

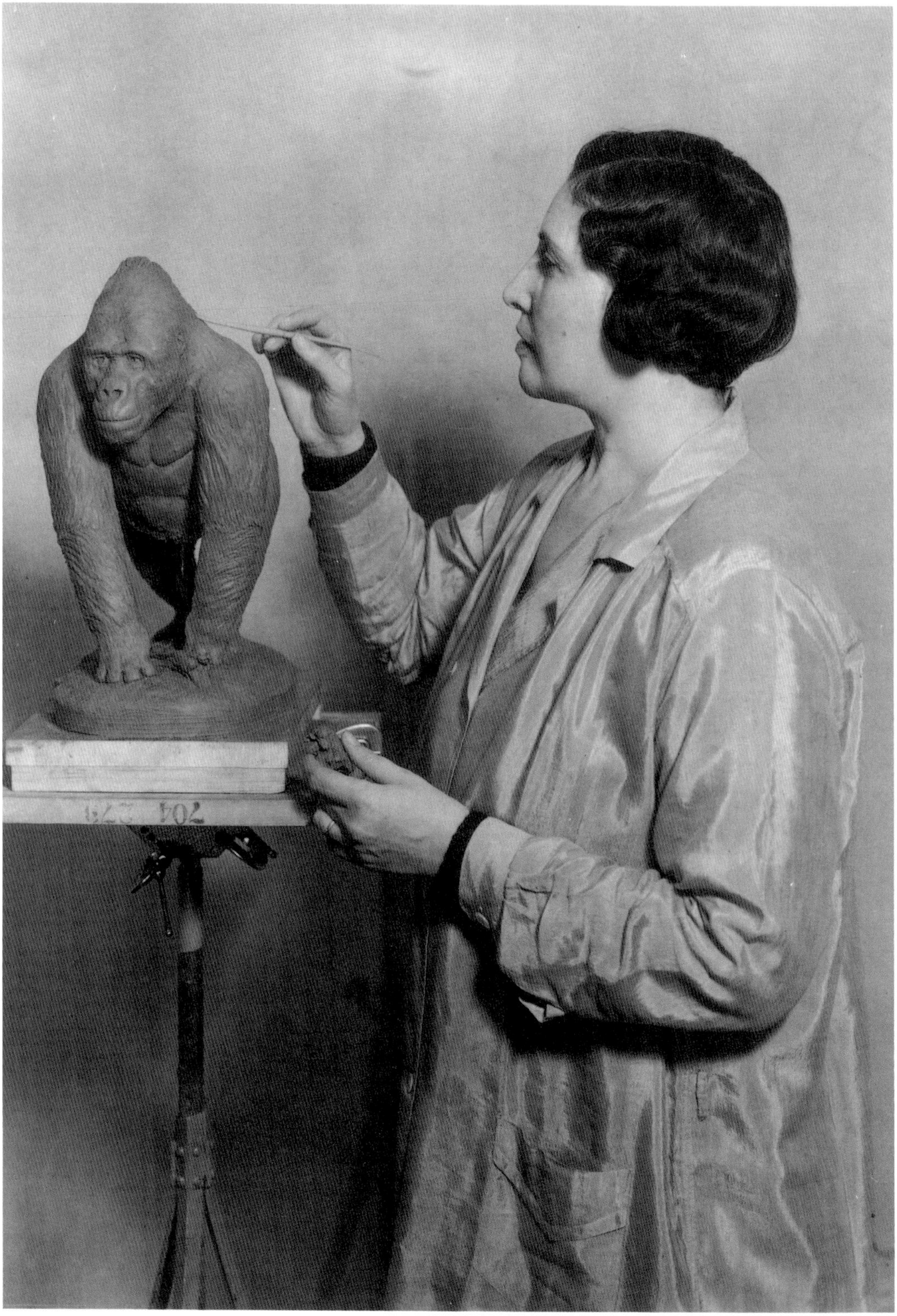

March

S	M	T	W	T	F	S
						1
2	3	4	5	6	7	8
9	10	11	12	13	14	15
16	17	18	19	20	21	22
23	24	25	26	27	28	29
30	31					

SALLY CLARK
(1883–1982)
Adventurer, sculptor

To peruse the early membership records of the Society of Woman Geographers (SWG) (acquired by the Library of Congress in 1988) is to witness an "old-girl network" of amazing reach and accomplishment. Founded in 1925 to bring together women active in exploration, geography, and allied disciplines, the SWG included among its members photographer Margaret Bourke-White, mountaineer Annie Smith Peck, anthropologist Margaret Mead, and many other intriguing women.

One such individual was the multifaceted Sally Clark, who after establishing a career as a clothing designer, married James L. Clark, creator of the animal exhibits at the American Museum of Natural History. Learning his trade, she soon became an accomplished hunter (though later she gave it up) and a recognized animal sculptor, taking part in expeditions to East Africa, the American West, Indochina, Canada, and Alaska. Clark also maintained a private studio where she portrayed notables of the day. She recorded her experiences in her autobiography, *From Lace to Lions*.

Society of Woman Geographers Collection
Manuscript Division

Artist and illustrator Kate Greenaway b. 1846

St. Patrick's Day

17 Monday — 76

Speed-skating champion Bonnie Blair b. 1964

18 Tuesday — 77

Comedian "Moms" Mabley b. 1897

19 Wednesday — 78

Yoko Ono marries John Lennon, 1969

Vernal Equinox 1:55 P.M. (GMT)

20 Thursday — 79

Debi Thomas becomes the first African American woman to win a gold medal in a world skating competition, 1986

21 Friday — 80

Poet Phyllis McGinley b. 1905

22 Saturday — 81

Virginia and Leonard Woolf establish the Hogarth Press, 1917

Palm Sunday

23 Sunday — 82

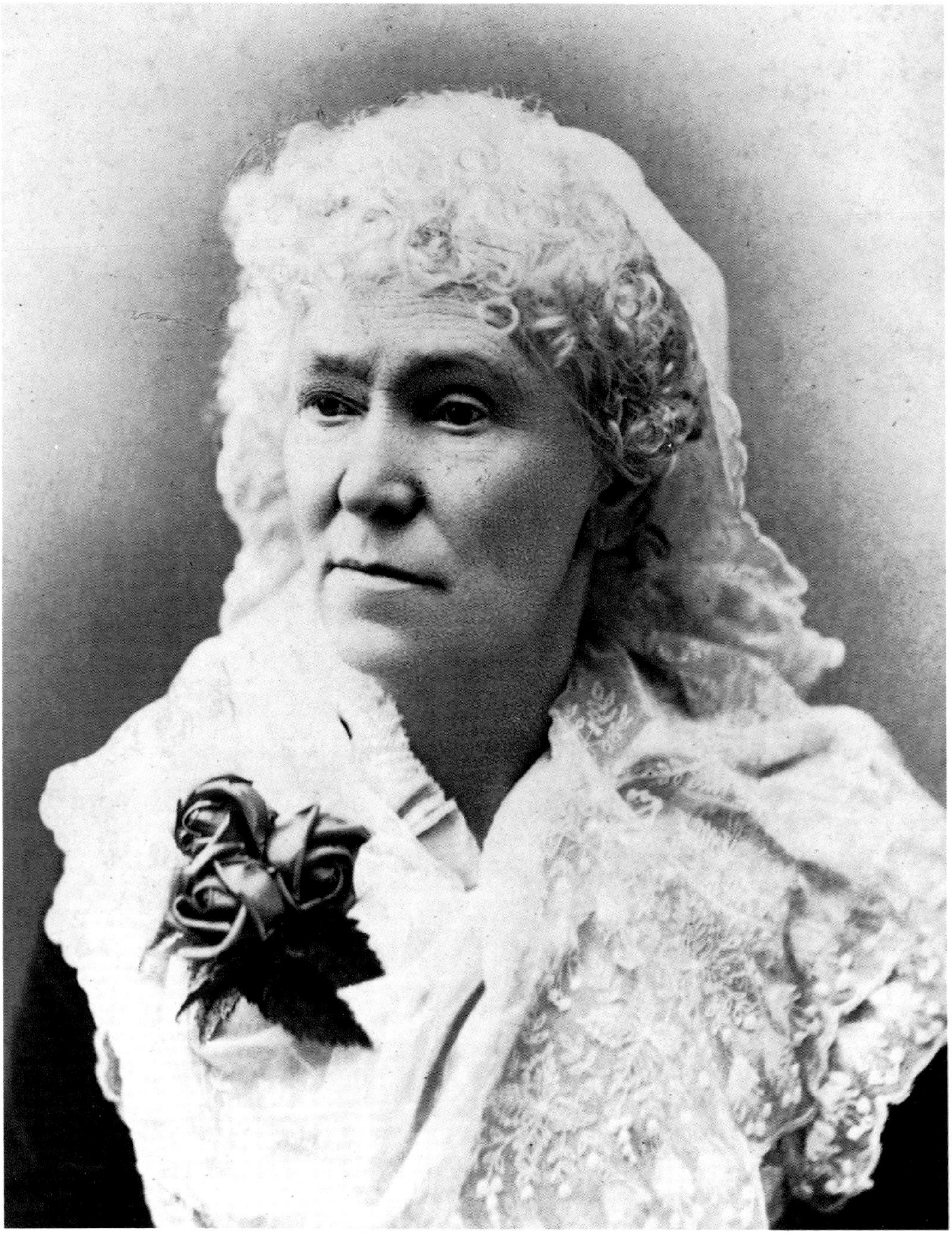

March

S	M	T	W	T	F	S
						1
2	3	4	5	6	7	8
9	10	11	12	13	14	15
16	17	18	19	20	21	22
23	24	25	26	27	28	29
30	31					

MATILDA JOSLYN GAGE
(1826–1898)
Suffragist, author

Our reform is everywhere advancing; let us redouble our energies and our courage.
    —Matilda Joslyn Gage and Susan B. Anthony, 1873

Strategist, organizer, editor, and writer, Matilda Joslyn Gage throughout her life lent a variety of crucial skills to the suffrage movement, even as her gentle demeanor and "feminine" appearance helped soften its radical image. In her first speech for women's rights in September 1852, she zeroed in on the economic and legal linchpins of women's inequality in society, urging that these be attacked by education as well as by political action. A longtime organizer and leader of the National Woman Suffrage Association, Gage also wrote for Susan Anthony's *Revolution,* edited the *National Citizen and Ballot Box,* and with Anthony and Elizabeth Cady Stanton produced the first three volumes of the NWSA's suffrage history. Increasingly she focused on the religious roots of gender bias, founding the Women's National Liberal Union, which advocated the separation of church and state, and producing the book *Woman, Church and State* (1893).

Prints and Photographs Division

Dorothy Stratton, director of the U.S. Coast Guard Women (SPARS) during World War II, b. 1899

Full Moon

24 Monday — 83

Suffragist Matilda Joslyn Gage b. 1826

25 Tuesday — 84

Louise Otto, German author and feminist pioneer, b. 1819

26 Wednesday — 85

Ruth Hanna McCormick, newspaper publisher and U.S. congresswoman, b. 1880

27 Thursday — 86

St. Teresa of Avila, influential mystic and author, b. 1515

Good Friday

28 Friday — 87

Author Judith Guest *(Ordinary People),* b. 1936

29 Saturday — 88

Pioneering psychologist Melanie Klein b. 1882

Easter Sunday

30 Sunday — 89

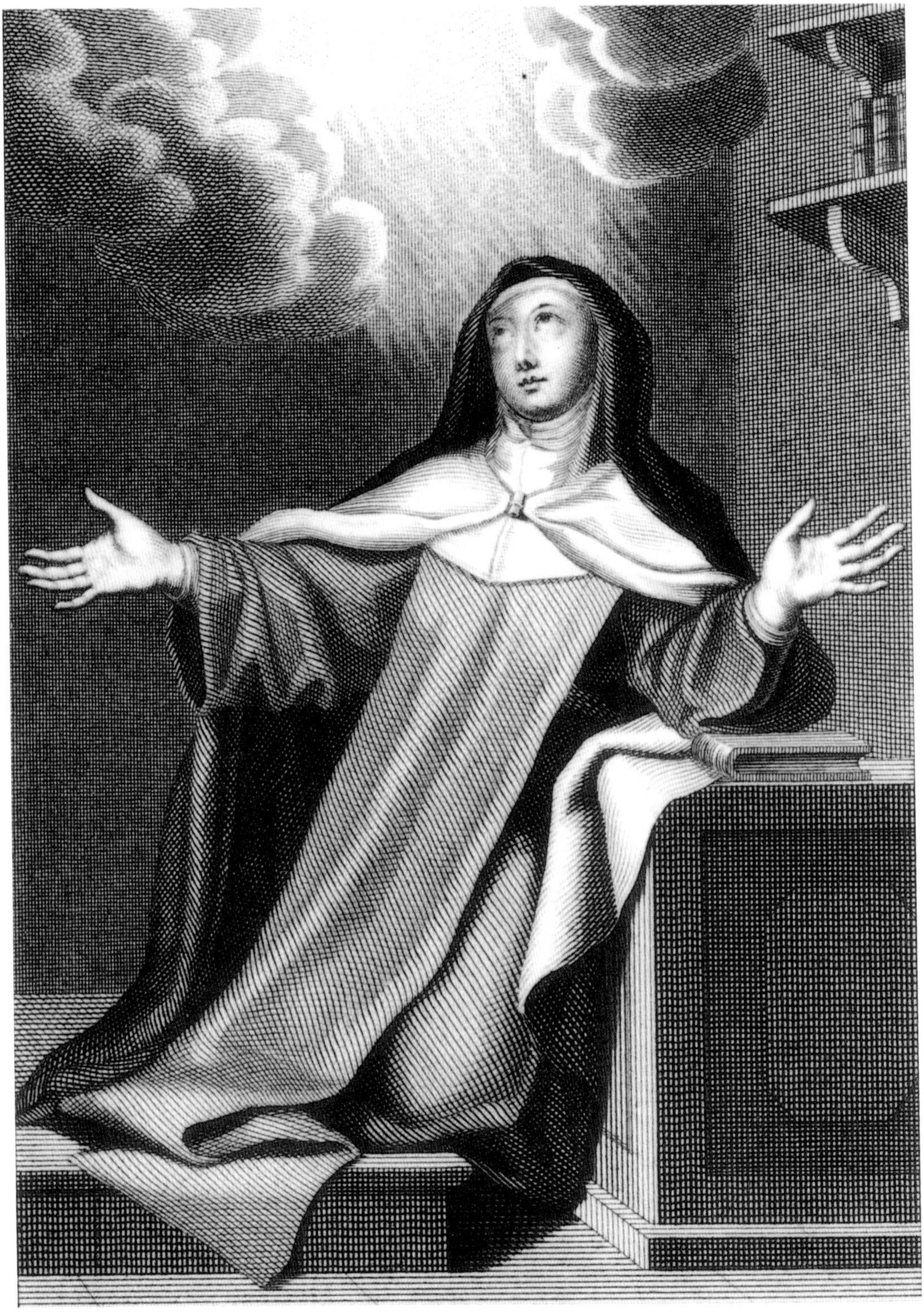

Mar/Apr

APRIL
S	M	T	W	T	F	S
		1	2	3	4	5
6	7	8	9	10	11	12
13	14	15	16	17	18	19
20	21	22	23	24	25	26
27	28	29	30			

TERESA OF AVILA
(1515–1582)
Mystic, writer

St. Teresa of Avila was arguably one of the most remarkable women of all time. Though she entered the religious life at an early age, she was nearly forty when she began having the visions that she later described in her book *Life* and that impelled her to found the Discalced Carmelites, an order whose strict discipline she believed would counteract some of the decadence of contemporary religious life. Controversy predictably swirled around her, but she successfully fought to maintain the safety of her new order with common sense, goodwill, and a sincere humility. A skillful and tireless manager, she traveled widely through Spain, establishing convents and houses for friars and, by action and example, reawakening spiritual impulses. Her written works—including *Interior Castle,* a glowing description of the contemplative life, and *Way of Perfection,* which provided instruction on prayer—are celebrated as literary masterworks.

General Collections

Abigail Adams writes to husband John, who is helping frame the Declaration of Independence: "Remember the ladies . . . [we] will not hold ourselves bound by any Laws in which we have no voice."

Easter Monday (Canada)
Last Quarter

31 Monday — 90

Wangari Maathai, Kenyan human rights and environmental activist, b. 1940

1 Tuesday — 91

Feminist scholar Barbara Caine *(Victorian Feminists)*, b. 1948

2 Wednesday — 92

Animal behaviorist Jane Goodall b. 1934

3 Thursday — 93

Author, actor, and journalist Maya Angelou b. 1928

4 Friday — 94

Catherine I, empress of Russia, b. 1684

5 Saturday — 95

Labor leader Rose Schneiderman b. 1884

6 Sunday — 96

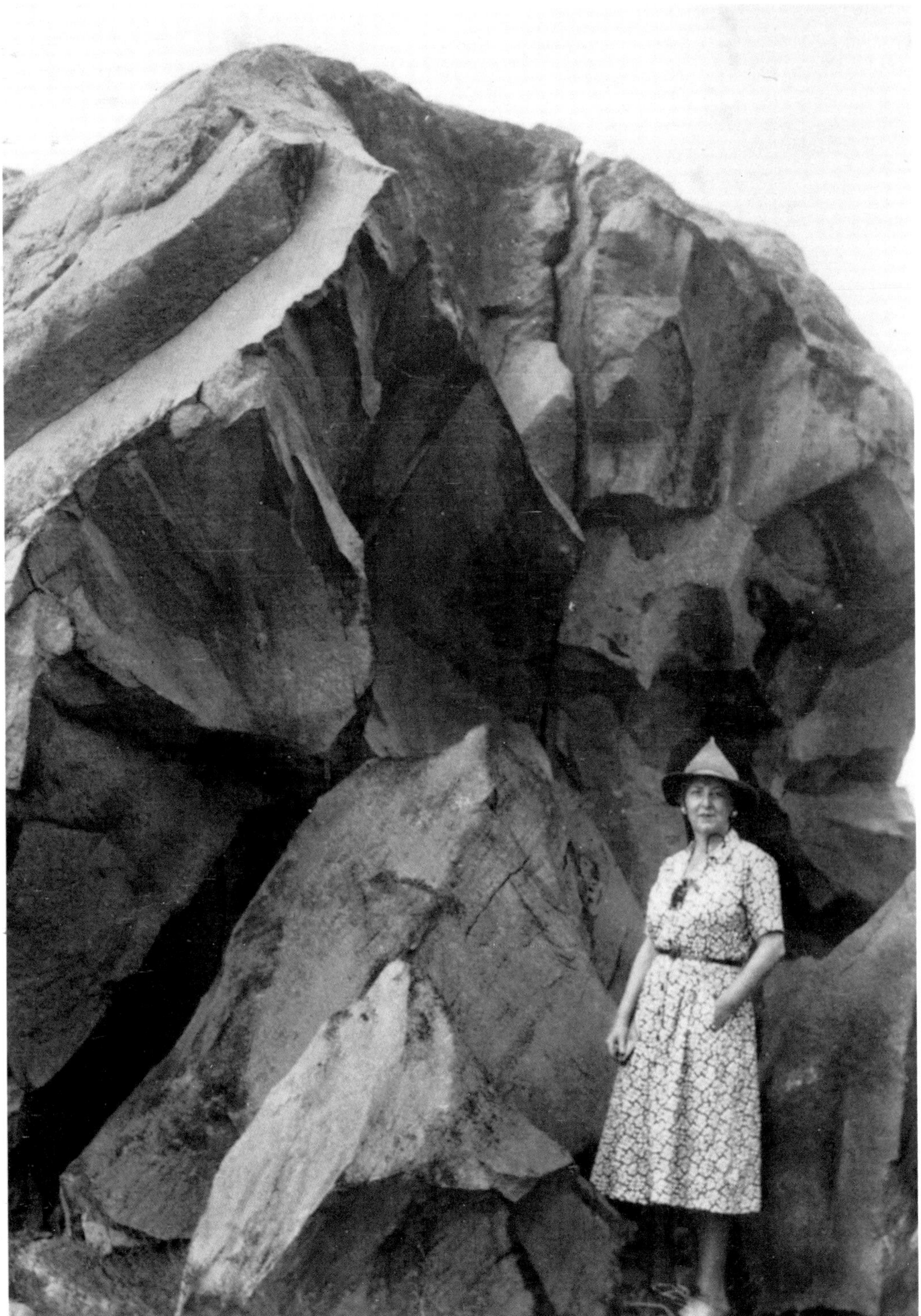

April

S	M	T	W	T	F	S
		1	2	3	4	5
6	7	8	9	10	11	12
13	14	15	16	17	18	19
20	21	22	23	24	25	26
27	28	29	30			

MARJORY STONEMAN DOUGLAS
(b. 1890)
Conservationist, writer

Marjory Stoneman Douglas, shown here in Martinique in 1945, is best known for her many years of writing and activism that have driven the grass roots conservationist movement in Florida. A native of Minnesota, Douglas graduated from Wellesley and moved to Florida in 1915, where she became a reporter for the *Miami Herald,* a newspaper founded and edited by her father. Though she covered a variety of beats, from society balls to World War I, it was her gift for description of flora and fauna, and her passion for her adopted land, that made her a force to be reckoned with. Her classic *Everglades: River of Grass* (1947) detailed the beauty of the Everglades and ended with a grim and prescient warning of its impending ruin. As founder and longtime head of the Friends of the Everglades, Douglas tirelessly challenged developers and the government to help preserve and restore that natural resource. In 1993, at age 103, Marjory Stoneman Douglas received the Medal of Freedom from President Clinton.

Society of Woman Geographers Collection
Manuscript Division

Everglades conservation activist Marjory Stoneman Douglas b. 1890

New Moon

7 Monday

Sonja Henie, world champion figure skater for ten consecutive years, b. 1913

8 Tuesday

Marie Luhring, first woman in the Society of Automotive Engineers, b. 1920

9 Wednesday

Women are first ordained as pastors in Sweden's Evangelical Lutheran Church, 1960

10 Thursday

Columnist Ellen Goodman b. 1941

11 Friday

Criminologist Eleanor Touroff Glueck b. 1883

12 Saturday

Pianist and composer Ethel Leginska b. 1886

13 Sunday

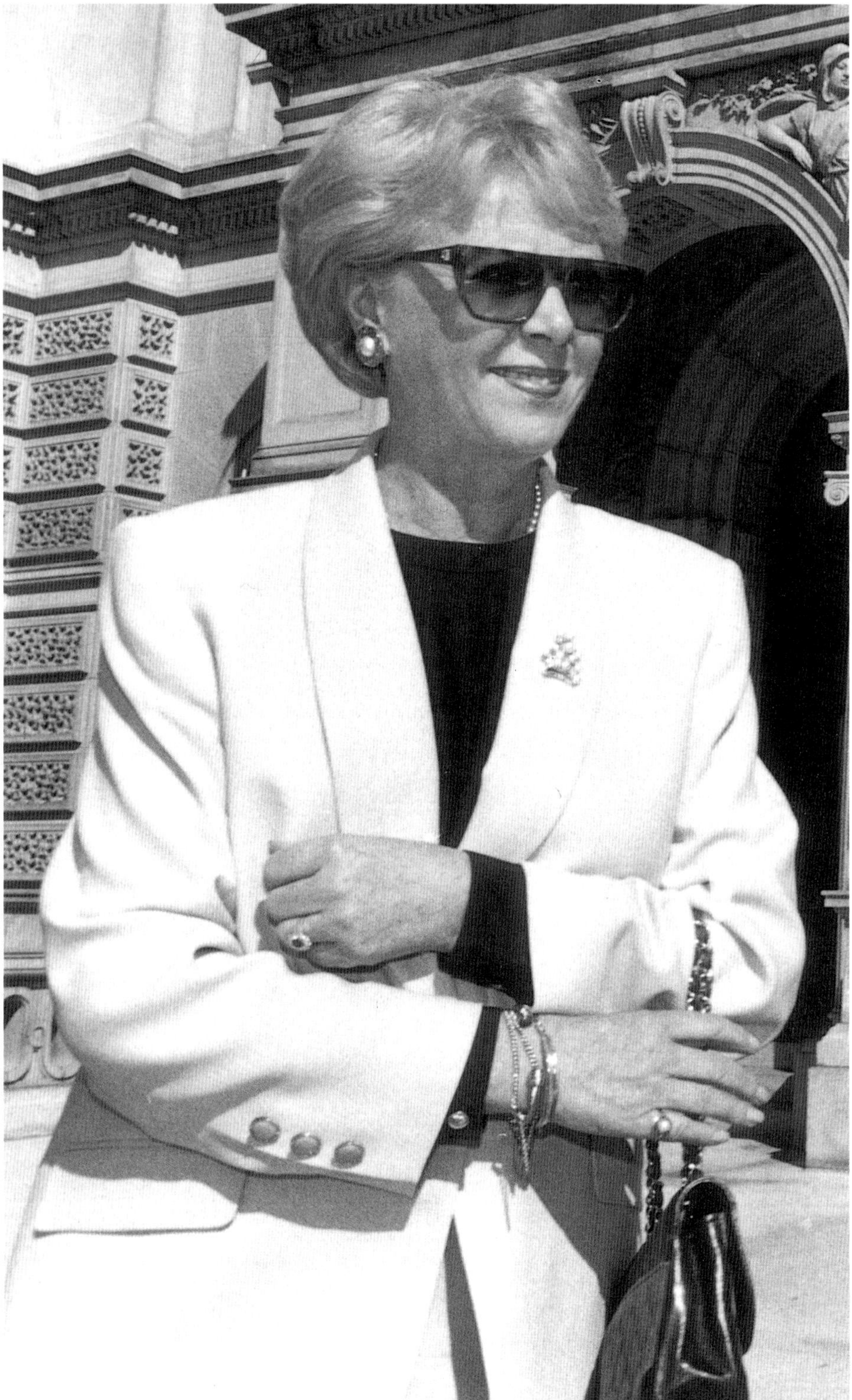

April

S	M	T	W	T	F	S
		1	2	3	4	5
6	7	8	9	10	11	12
13	14	15	16	17	18	19
20	21	22	23	24	25	26
27	28	29	30			

VIGDÍS FINNBOGADÓTTIR
(b. 1930)
President of Iceland

Vigdís Finnbogadóttir, shown here during a 1991 visit to the Library of Congress, is the first woman in recorded history to be democratically elected as a constitutional head of state. In Iceland the president exercises authority via ministers, thus remaining above politics while wielding considerable influence and serving to personify national unity. "President Vigdís," as everyone in Iceland calls her, was first elected in 1980 and has been thrice reelected as of this writing. A native of Reykjavík, with a career that has encompassed realms from theater to education, Finnbogadóttir has sought to foster cultural connection over political division, both inside and outside her country. She has also become an ambassador for women everywhere, speaking out for "parity democracy"—50 percent of governmental decision makers being women—at the Fourth World Conference on Women in Beijing in 1995. Her adoption of a baby daughter in 1972 was one of the first instances of a single person in her country adopting a child.
Photograph by Jim Higgins
Library of Congress

Anne Mansfield Sullivan, teacher of Helen Keller, b. 1866

First Quarter

14 Monday — 104

Vigdís Finnbogadóttir, president of Iceland, b. 1930

15 Tuesday — 105

Beverly Kelley becomes the first female commander of a Coast Guard ship, 1979

16 Wednesday — 106

Editor and pioneer penologist Isabel Barrows b. 1845

17 Thursday — 107

Women's World Fair opens in Chicago, 1925

18 Friday — 108

Diarist and businesswoman Sarah Kemble Knight b. 1666

19 Saturday — 109

New Zealand–born American Helen Thayer, traveling on foot and on skis, reaches the North Pole with her sole companion, a husky, 1988

20 Sunday — 110

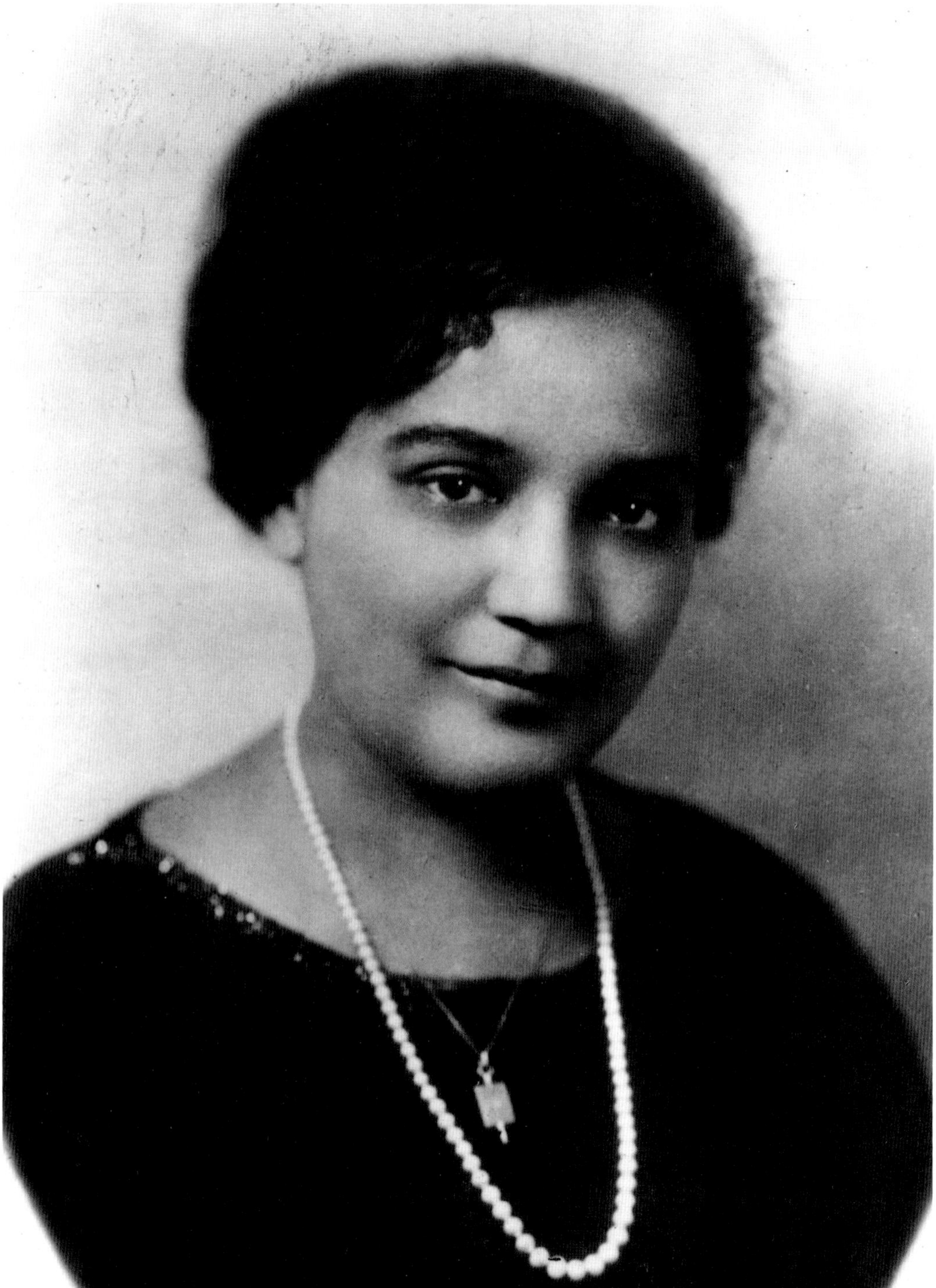

April

S	M	T	W	T	F	S
		1	2	3	4	5
6	7	8	9	10	11	12
13	14	15	16	17	18	19
20	21	22	23	24	25	26
27	28	29	30			

JESSIE REDMON FAUSET
(1882–1861)
Writer

As literary editor of the NAACP's *Crisis* magazine (1919–1926), Jessie Redmon Fauset was one of three people Langston Hughes credited with "mid-wif[ing] the so-called New Negro literature into being. Kind and critical . . . they nursed us along until our books were born." Fauset, among the first African Americans to graduate (Phi Beta Kappa) from Cornell University, nursed along books of her own as well. She produced four novels dominated by a single theme: the fundamental importance of human relationships in a world rife with racial and sexual barriers. They were written in the midst of other jobs and other writing (poetry, essays, magazine articles, and material for the children's magazine *The Brownies' Book,* which she also edited), a fact that moved her to tell one interviewer of her longing to devote a year or two solely to a novel, "just to see what I really could do if I had my full time and energy to devote to my work."

Harmon Foundation Collection
Manuscript Division

Author, professor of theology, and Methodist pastor Rev. Dr. Georgia Elma Harkness b. 1891

Passover
(begins at sundown)

21 Monday — 111

Rita Levi-Montalcini, Italian neurobiologist and Nobel laureate, b. 1909

Earth Day
Full Moon

22 Tuesday — 112

Dame Edith Ngaio March, one of New Zealand's most popular authors, creator of Scotland Yard inspector Roderick Allen, b. 1899

23 Wednesday — 113

Singer, actor, and director Barbra Streisand b. 1942

24 Thursday — 114

Jazz great Ella Fitzgerald b. 1918

25 Friday — 115

Sybil Ludington, age 16, rides through towns in New York and Connecticut warning citizens of advancing British troops and amassing resistance, 1777

26 Saturday — 116

Author and editor Jessie Redmon Fauset b. 1882

27 Sunday — 117

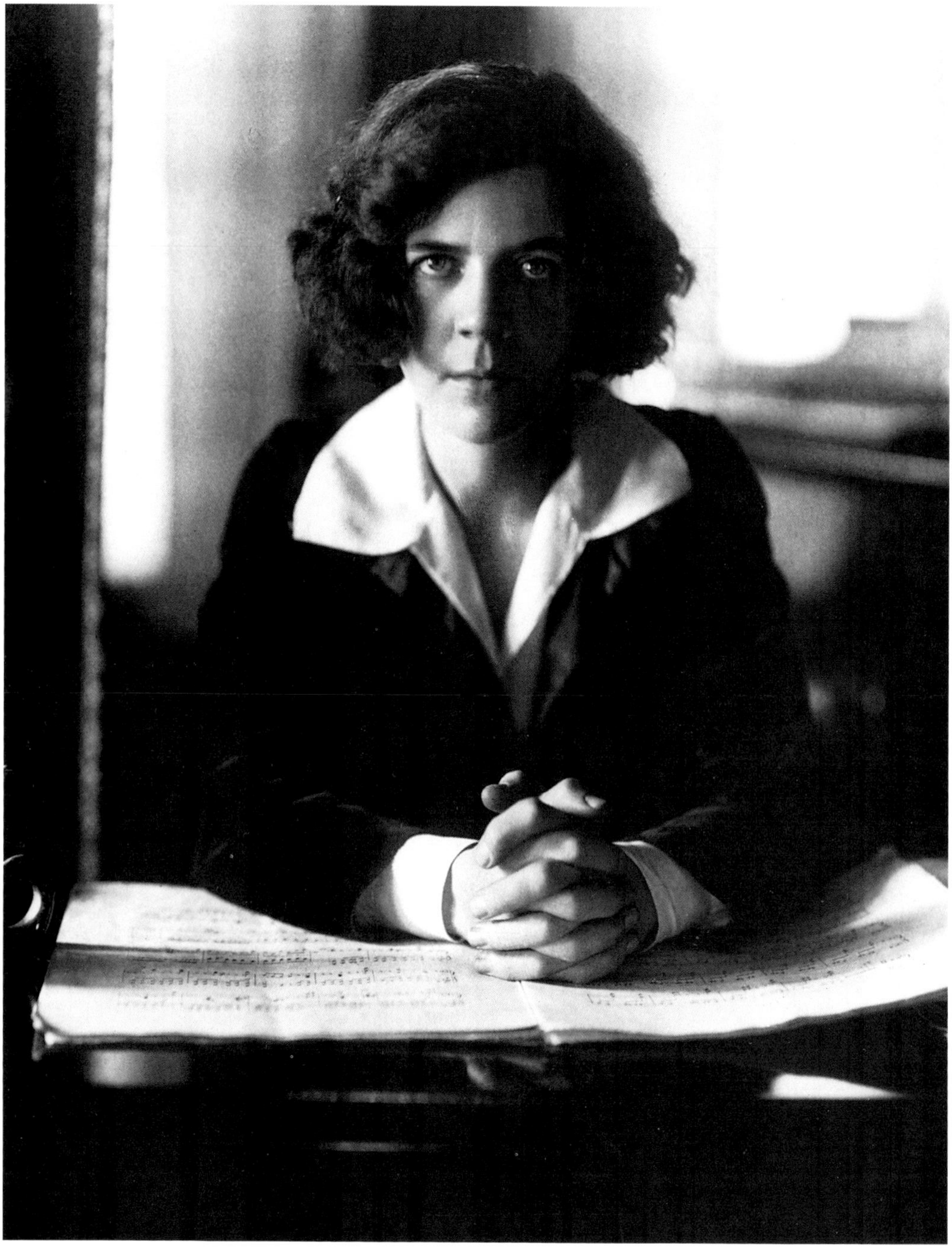

Apr/May

MAY						
S	M	T	W	T	F	S
				1	2	3
4	5	6	7	8	9	10
11	12	13	14	15	16	17
18	19	20	21	22	23	24
25	26	27	28	29	30	31

ETHEL LEGINSKA
(1886–1970)
Pianist, composer

Naturally talented in music from childhood, Ethel Leginska made a career as a concert pianist and composer—but made history in her principal avocational interest, conducting. Born in Hull, England, Leginska studied piano in Frankfurt and Vienna before debuting in London in 1907. After successfully touring Europe she came to the United States in 1913, where critics used words like "dashing" and "masculine vigor" to describe her playing. Amid her performing career she became increasingly interested in conducting. This led to her forming the one hundred–piece Boston Philharmonic Orchestra (later the Women's Symphony Orchestra of Boston) and guest-conducting a number of orchestras in the United States and Europe, blazing a new trail of female visibility on the podium. Leginska the composer studied with Ernest Bloch, and her works (including two operas, symphonic pieces, and a string quartet after four poems of Tagore) are an intriguing blend of traditional and modernist elements.

Coolidge Foundation Collection
Music Division

Singer and pianist Blossom Dearie b. 1926

28 Monday — 118

Florence Sabin becomes the first woman elected to the National Academy of Sciences, 1925

29 Tuesday — 119

Actor Eve Arden, "Our Miss Brooks," b. 1912

Last Quarter

30 Wednesday — 120

Gwendolyn Brooks becomes the first African American woman to win the Pulitzer Prize in poetry, 1950

1 Thursday — 121

Catherine II ("the Great") of Russia, one of the most influential rulers in Western history, b. 1729

2 Friday — 122

Belva Lockwood, after successfully lobbying Congress to end gender apartheid at the bar of the U.S. Supreme Court, becomes the first woman to argue before that court, 1879

3 Saturday — 123

Anna Chandy, first female judge in India, b. 1905

4 Sunday — 124

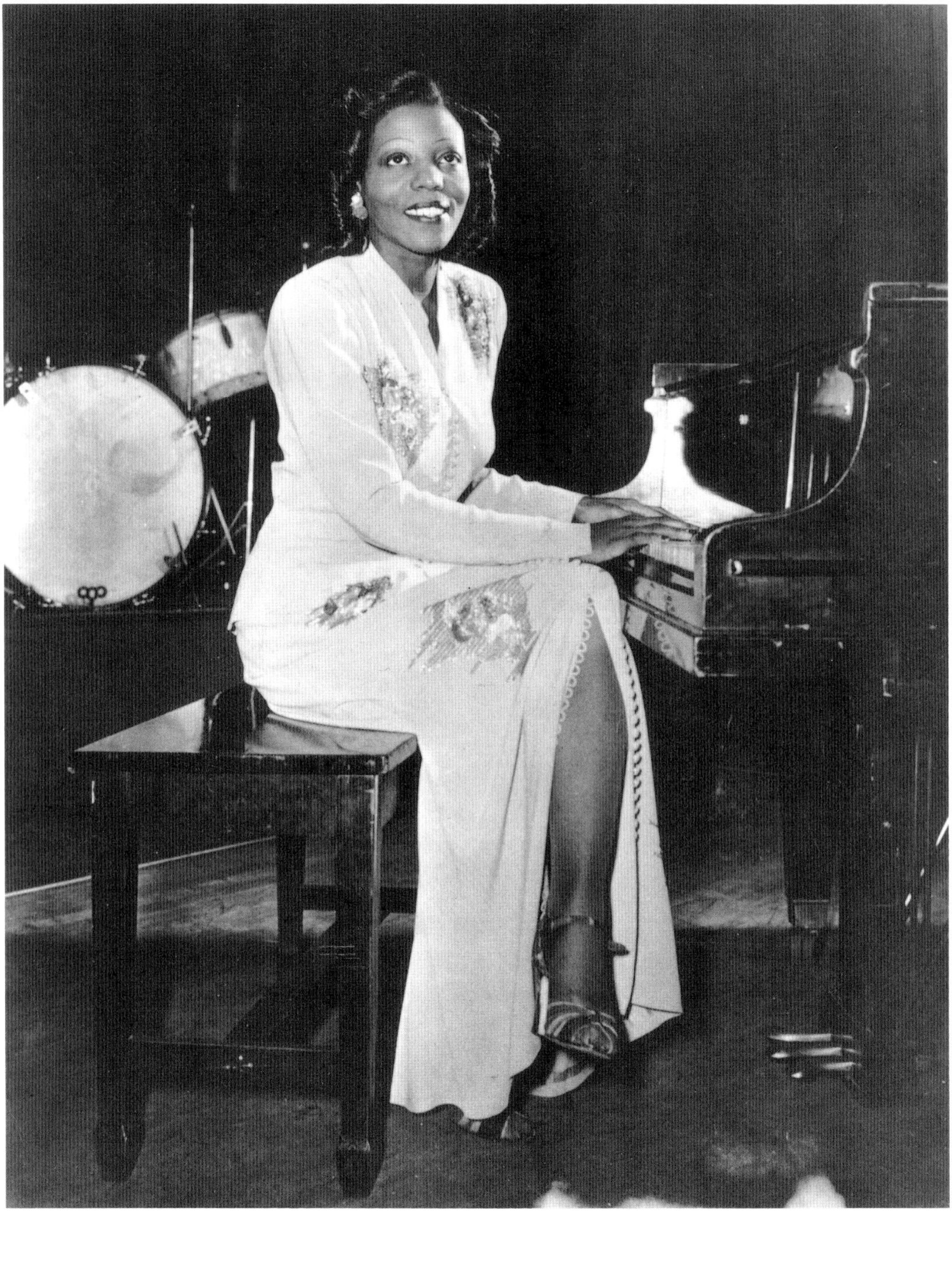

May

S	M	T	W	T	F	S
				1	2	3
4	5	6	7	8	9	10
11	12	13	14	15	16	17
18	19	20	21	22	23	24
25	26	27	28	29	30	31

MARY LOU WILLIAMS
(1910–1981)
Pianist, composer, arranger, educator

Mary Lou Williams grew up in a home where her prodigious natural gifts were recognized and nurtured, and the rich musical landscape beyond provided constant inspiration. Seeing pianist-arranger Lovie Austin perform had a particular impact; Williams later recalled Austin "playing with her left hand, writing music for the next act with the other . . . and conducting the band with her head. Although I was just a little baby, I said to myself, 'I'm going to do that one day.'" Williams did that and much more, from her earliest professional performances at age twelve through her seminal contributions to the bluesy, driving "Kansas City swing" style of big-band jazz, as a champion of bebop and its early innovators, and as a composer whose works encompassed almost every style of twentieth-century music. Long known as "the First Lady of Jazz," Williams later taught at Duke University and the University of Massachusetts.

New York World-Telegram and Sun Collection
Prints and Photographs Division

---

5 Monday — 125
Dr. Dorothy H. Andersen identifies the disease cystic fibrosis, 1938

Cinco de Mayo

6 Tuesday — 126
Phebe Hanaford, author and Universalist minister, b. 1829

New Moon

7 Wednesday — 127
Ruth Prawer Jhabvala, Anglo-Indian author and screenwriter, b. 1927

8 Thursday — 128
Mary Lou Williams, "First Lady of Jazz," b. 1910

9 Friday — 129
Journalist, author, and musician Philippa Duke Schuyler dies in a helicopter crash in Vietnam, 1967

10 Saturday — 130
Dancer and choreographer Judith Jameson b. 1944

11 Sunday — 131
Dancer and choreographer Martha Graham b. 1893

Mother's Day

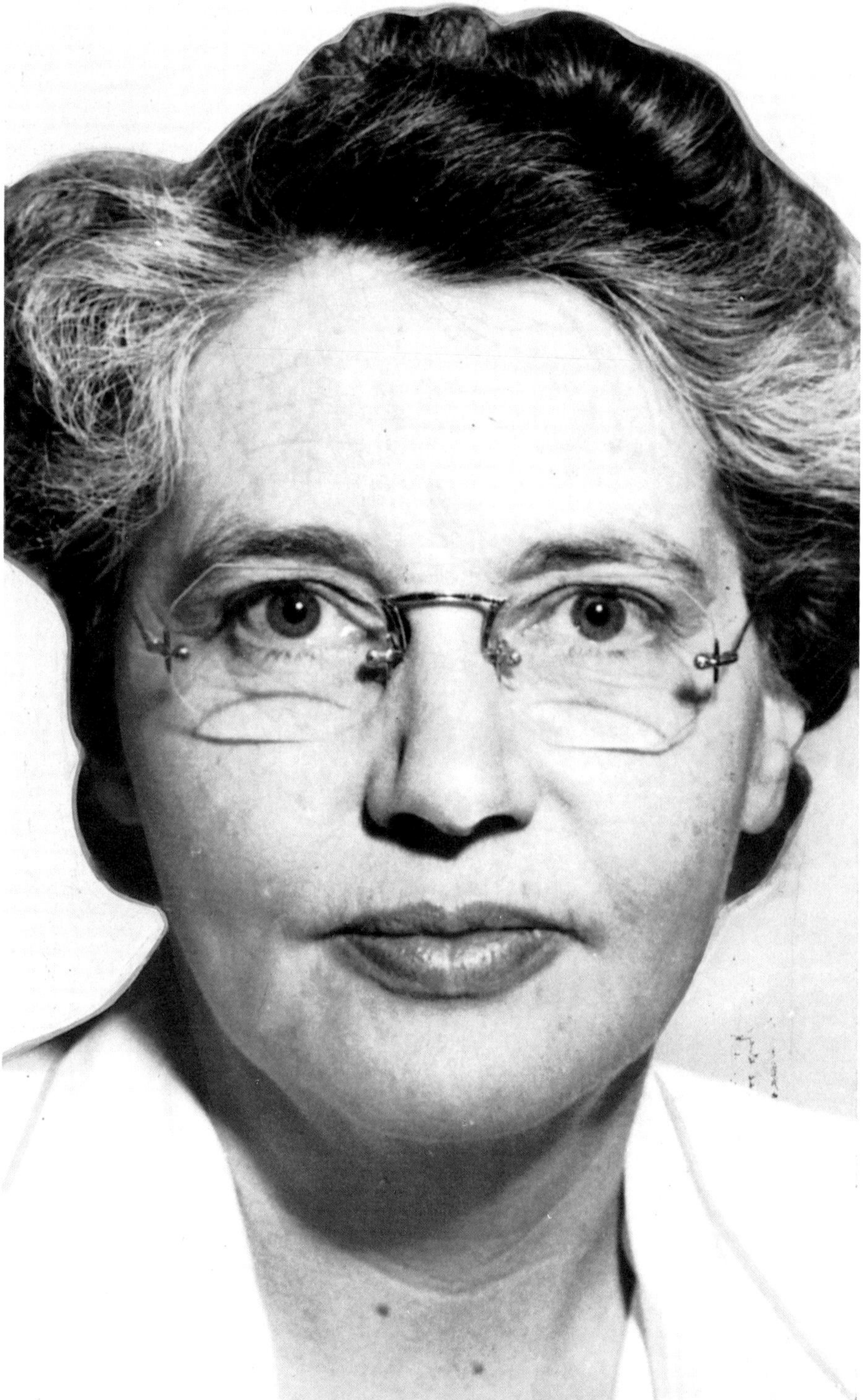

May

S	M	T	W	T	F	S
				1	2	3
4	5	6	7	8	9	10
11	12	13	14	15	16	17
18	19	20	21	22	23	24
25	26	27	28	29	30	31

HELEN BROOKE TAUSSIG
(1898–1986)
Cardiologist, professor

Having struggled with severe dyslexia to complete college, Helen Brooke Taussig regarded the fact that women were rarely admitted to medical school as just another hurdle to get past. She completed her studies at Johns Hopkins Medical School—but was then confronted with the loss of her hearing. Determined to practice anyway, and choosing pediatric cardiology as her specialty, she learned to read lips and to "listen with her fingers" to her patients' hearts. This fine-tuned sensitivity, combined with her acute powers of observation, led Taussig to one of the most important discoveries in cardiac care in the twentieth century—and to the beginning of open-heart surgery. Babies were once routinely born with cyanosis; the so-called blue babies generally died very young. It was Taussig who determined that a lack of oxygen was the cause of the disorder. She developed a successful surgical technique to correct the problem, and soon cyanosis, a killer disease, was virtually wiped out.

New York World-Telegram and Sun Collection
Prints and Photographs Division

Sharon S. Adams leaves Yokohama, Japan, on the first solo transpacific crossing by a woman, 1969

132
12
Monday

Author Daphne Du Maurier b. 1907

133
13
Tuesday

Mary Williams, who helped resolve boundary disputes between Honduras, Guatemala, and Nicaragua, b. 1878

First Quarter

134
14
Wednesday

Mary Kies becomes the first U.S. woman granted a patent (for "a new and useful improvement in weaving straw with silk or thread"), 1809

135
15
Thursday

Anthropologist Mary Thygeson Shepardson b. 1906

136
16
Friday

U.S. Energy Secretary Hazel O'Leary b. 1937

Armed Forces Day

137
17
Saturday

Aviator Jackie Cochran breaks the sound barrier, 1953

138
18
Sunday

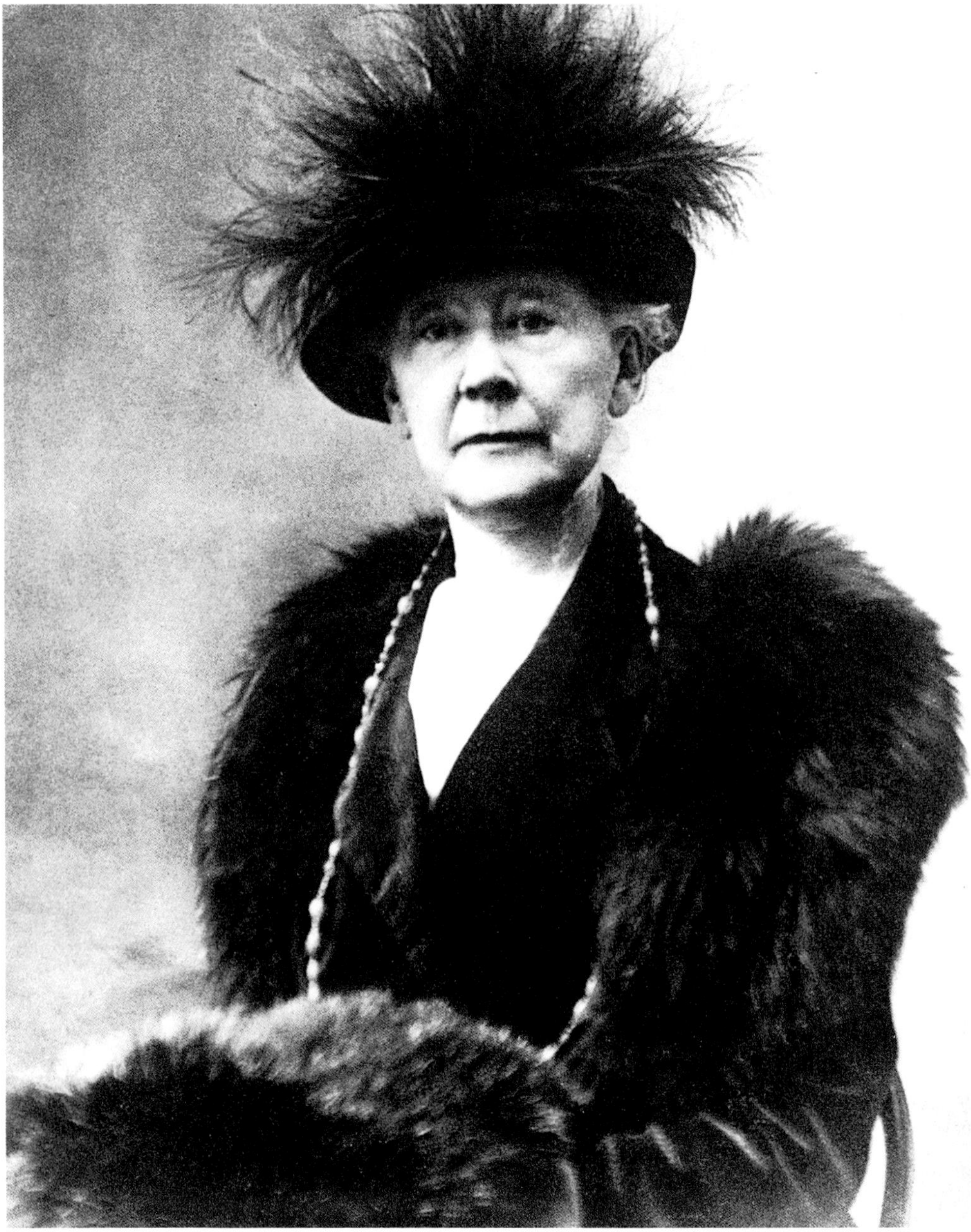

May

S	M	T	W	T	F	S
				1	2	3
4	5	6	7	8	9	10
11	12	13	14	15	16	17
18	19	20	21	22	23	24
25	26	27	28	29	30	31

MARY STEVENSON CASSATT (1844–1926)
Artist

The only American painter to win acceptance into the elite circle of French Impressionists, Mary Stevenson Cassatt got her first taste of Europe, and most significantly of Paris, as a young girl during her family's travels. When as a girl she announced her desire to be a painter, her father said he would sooner see her dead. She, however, prevailed, studying at the Pennsylvania Academy of the Fine Arts in Philadelphia from 1861 to 1864, and then settling in Paris. Her work caught the attention of Edgar Degas, who became an important influence (along with Japanese printmakers). Cassatt's oils and pastels, usually featuring unsentimental depictions of women and children, brought her fame by the 1880s, and her attendant efforts—such as encouraging the purchase and exhibition of European art in the United States—made her an important cultural force as well. "One does not need to follow the lessons of an instructor," she said; "the lessons of museums are enough." Mary Cassatt's life and artistic achievements, however, continue to instruct and inspire the many female artists whose stature she did so much to raise.

General Collections

Australian soprano Dame Nellie Melba b. 1861

Victoria Day (Canada)

19 Monday — 139

Norwegian novelist Sigrid Undset (1928 Nobel laureate in literature) b. 1882

20 Tuesday — 140

Frances Densmore, ethnomusicologist who recorded songs of Native Americans, b. 1867

21 Wednesday — 141

Impressionist painter Mary Stevenson Cassatt b. 1844

Full Moon

22 Thursday — 142

Margaret Fuller, nineteenth-century intellectual extraordinaire, b. 1810

23 Friday — 143

Helen Taussig, physician who diagnosed the cause of "blue babies," b. 1898

24 Saturday — 144

Mme. C. J. Walker, first self-made female millionaire in U.S., d. 1919

25 Sunday — 145

SILENT SPRING
MAN'S ROLE
IN CHANGIN
THE FACE OF
THE EARTH
GOOD READING
SEEING AMERICA'S WILDLIFE
William O. Douglas
Creatures of the Night
THE SQUEEZE
Justice Holmes
Insects
THE EARTH

May/Jun

JUNE
S	M	T	W	T	F	S
	1	2	3	4	5	6	7
8	9	10	11	12	13	14
15	16	17	18	19	20	21
22	23	24	25	26	27	28
29	30

RACHEL CARSON
(1907–1964)
Biologist, author

Rachel Carson made a successful career combining the interests of her youth—science and literature—as a marine biologist, editor for the U.S. Fish and Wildlife Service, and best-selling author of books such as *The Sea Around Us* (1951). The lyrical, explosive *Silent Spring* (1962), completed with heroic effort as Carson battled cancer, brought unprecedented attention to the dangers of indiscriminate use of chemical pesticides and was a prime catalyst of the U.S. environmental movement in the latter half of the twentieth century. Though the pesticide industry reacted to *Silent Spring* by attempting to discredit Carson and her findings, she coolly and firmly continued to speak out on the need to temper technological progress with a broader view of its effects. The 1995 volume *Always, Rachel* (Beacon Press), a collection of letters between Carson and longtime friend Dorothy Freeman, movingly depicts Carson's exhilaration at the "fabric of life" around her, as well as a uniquely deep relationship between like-minded women.

New York World-Telegram and Sun Collection
Prints and Photographs Division

Sally Ride, physicist and first U.S. woman in space, b. 1951

Memorial Day (Observed)

146
26
Monday

Biologist and author Rachel Carson b. 1907

147
27
Tuesday

Poet May Swenson b. 1919

148
28
Wednesday

Elizabeth Pringle, South Carolina plantation owner and author, b. 1845

Last Quarter

149
29
Thursday

Astronomer Maria Mitchell becomes the first woman elected to the American Academy of Arts and Sciences, 1848

Memorial Day

150
30
Friday

Mary Hannah Fulton, founder of the Hackett Medical College for Women in Canton, China, b. 1854

151
31
Saturday

Mme. Adolphe becomes the first woman to perform on a tightrope in the U.S., New York City, 1819

152
1
Sunday

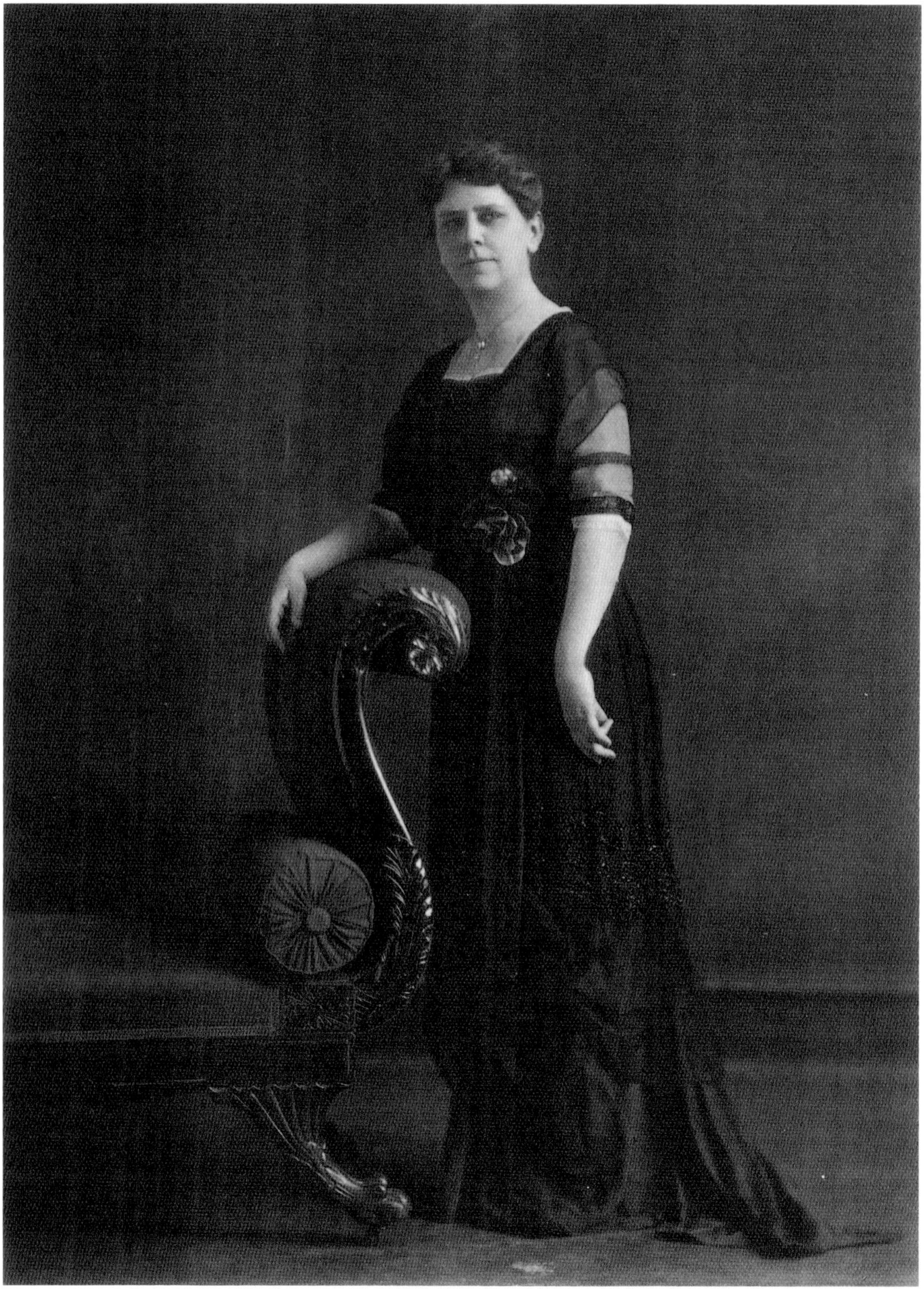

June

S	M	T	W	T	F	S
1	2	3	4	5	6	7
8	9	10	11	12	13	14
15	16	17	18	19	20	21
22	23	24	25	26	27	28
29	30					

FRANCES DENSMORE
(1867–1957)
Ethnomusicologist

One of the most active and important of the early U.S. ethnomusicologists, Frances Densmore devoted her long career to preserving the musical heritage of the American Indian. As a child in Red Wing, Minnesota, she had heard the songs of the Sioux drift over the prairie at night. Those voices stayed with her through years of studying and teaching music, drawing her at last to her life's work. In 1907 Densmore began a long association with the Smithsonian Institution, whose Bureau of American Ethnology gave her a grant of $150 to study American Indian music. The Edison phonograph she bought with the money was the most important tool she used to help document a priceless body of song that was beginning to disappear. Eventually she recorded the songs of more than thirty tribes. Densmore's deep respect for the people she documented was rewarded in kind; in 1911, Red Fox of the Sioux Indians named her Two White Buffalo Woman and adopted her as a daughter. Most photographs of Densmore show her in the field; this unusual formal photograph is from lecture materials she donated to the Library of Congress.

Frances Densmore Collection
Music Division

African American novelist Dorothy West b. 1907

2 Monday — 153

Entertainer and activist Josephine Baker b. 1906

3 Tuesday — 154

Carson McCullers, age 23, publishes *The Heart Is a Lonely Hunter* to critical acclaim, 1940

4 Wednesday — 155

Native Hawaiian feminist Kaahumanu d. 1832

New Moon

5 Thursday — 156

Marian Wright Edelman, founder of the Children's Defense Fund, b. 1939

6 Friday — 157

Writer and activist Nikki Giovanni b. 1943

7 Saturday — 158

Mystery writer Sara Paretsky b. 1947

8 Sunday — 159

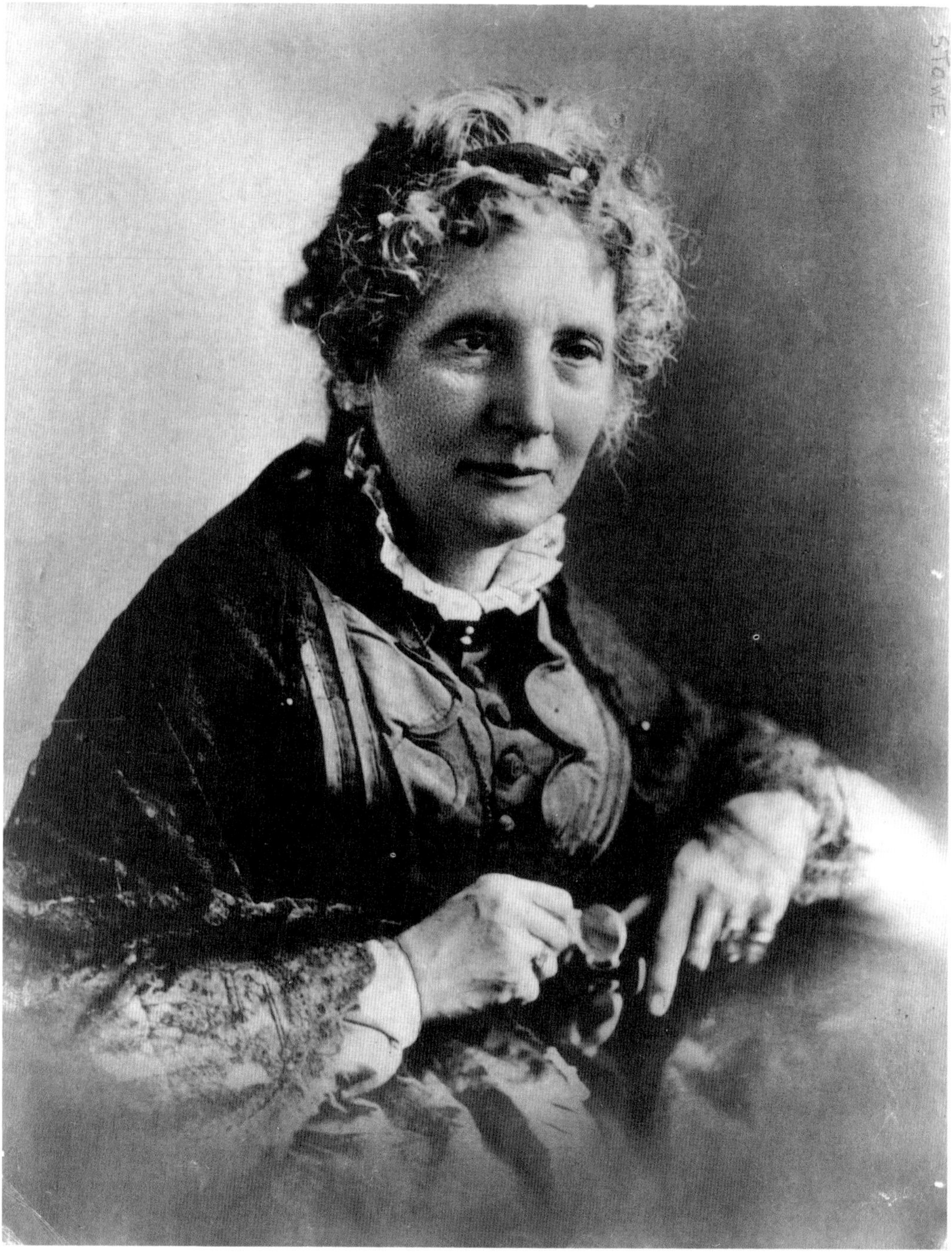
STOWE

June

S	M	T	W	T	F	S
	1	2	3	4	5	6	7
8	9	10	11	12	13	14
15	16	17	18	19	20	21
22	23	24	25	26	27	28
29	30

HARRIET BEECHER STOWE
(1811–1896)
Novelist

"Art as an end, not instrument, has little to interest me," Harriet Beecher Stowe wrote to George Eliot. Wife of a theology professor and mother of seven, Stowe was a woman of determination, whimsy, strength, common sense, loyalty to people and ideals, and remarkable intelligence ("Hattie," her father said, "is a genius"). These traits, and her sense of purpose, characterized her many short stories, travel books, poetry, essays, domestic manuals, and novels. An enemy of slavery, Stowe was the first American writer to conceive a novel with a black man as the hero. *Uncle Tom's Cabin, or Life Among the Lowly* (1852) became one of the most influential books of the nineteenth century, bringing its author instant fame as well as tremendous acrimony from slavery's supporters. It far overshadows the other books she subsequently produced at the rate of almost one per year. Among the best of these are *The Pearl of Orr's Island* (1862), *The Minister's Wooing* (1859), and *Oldtown Folks* (1868).

Prints and Photographs Division

160
Georgia Neese Clark is confirmed as first female treasurer of the U.S., 1949

9
Monday

161
Bridget Bishop becomes the first of the Salem "witches" to be hanged, 1692

10
Tuesday

162
English photographer Julia Margaret Cameron b. 1815

11
Wednesday

163
Babe Didrikson Zaharias becomes the first U.S. woman to win the British Women's Amateur Golf Tournament, 1947

12
Thursday

164
Mystery writer and classicist Dorothy L. Sayers b. 1893

First Quarter

13
Friday

165
Novelist Harriet Beecher Stowe b. 1811

Flag Day

14
Saturday

166
Malvina Hoffman, sculptor who created 110 life-size figures for the Field Museum of Chicago, b. 1887

Father's Day

15
Sunday

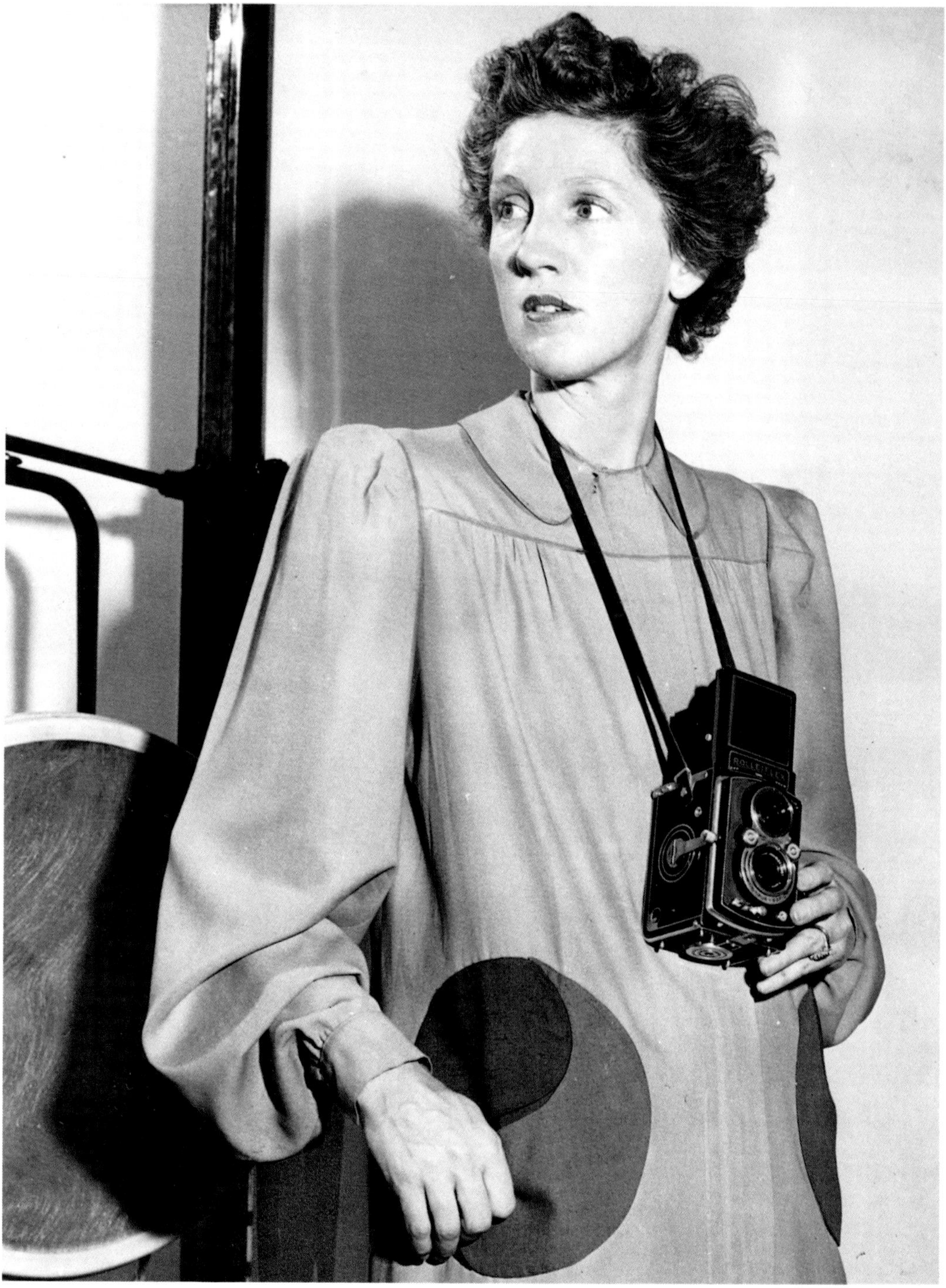
ROLLEIFLEX

June

S	M	T	W	T	F	S
1	2	3	4	5	6	7
8	9	10	11	12	13	14
15	16	17	18	19	20	21
22	23	24	25	26	27	28
29	30					

TONI FRISSELL
(1907–1988)
Photographer

Toni Frissell began her career as a professional photographer in 1931, creating fashion spreads for *Vogue* magazine. By the time she retired, in the early 1970s, Frissell had adventured in—and left a lasting mark on—photographic arenas from high society to combat to sports. Introduced to cameras by her brother, a news photographer for the Pathé film company, Frissell quickly made her mark at *Vogue* by taking her models outdoors and posing them amid craggy seascapes, ruins, and other sweeping exteriors. After eleven years at *Vogue* she covered high society for *Harper's Bazaar*. During World War II she elbowed her way to the European front, where she covered subjects from the Women's Army Corps (WACs) to the 332nd Fighter Pilot Squadron led by Benjamin O. Davis. After the war Frissell's interest turned to sports, and her enormous variety of work for *Sports Illustrated* left a lasting impact on the look and style of that magazine. This photograph shows Frissell circa 1940, gamely allowing the tables to be turned as she models a new suit for a promotion.

New York World-Telegram and Sun Collection
Prints and Photographs Division

Junko Tabei becomes the first woman to reach the summit of Mt. Everest, 1975

167
16
Monday

Susan La Flesche Picotte, Omaha Indian physician, b. 1865

168
17
Tuesday

Susan B. Anthony, fined $100 for "illegal voting," informs the judge she will never pay it (she never did), 1873

169
18
Wednesday

Aung San Suu Kyi, Burmese human rights leader and Nobel Peace Prize laureate, b. 1945

170
19
Thursday

Queen Victoria of England begins her 64-year reign, 1837

Full Moon

171
20
Friday

Novelist and dramatist Françoise Sagan *(Bonjour Tristesse)* b. 1935

Summer Solstice 8:20 A.M. (GMT)

172
21
Saturday

Alice Gertrude Bryand and Florence West Duckering become the first women admitted to the American College of Surgeons, 1914

173
22
Sunday

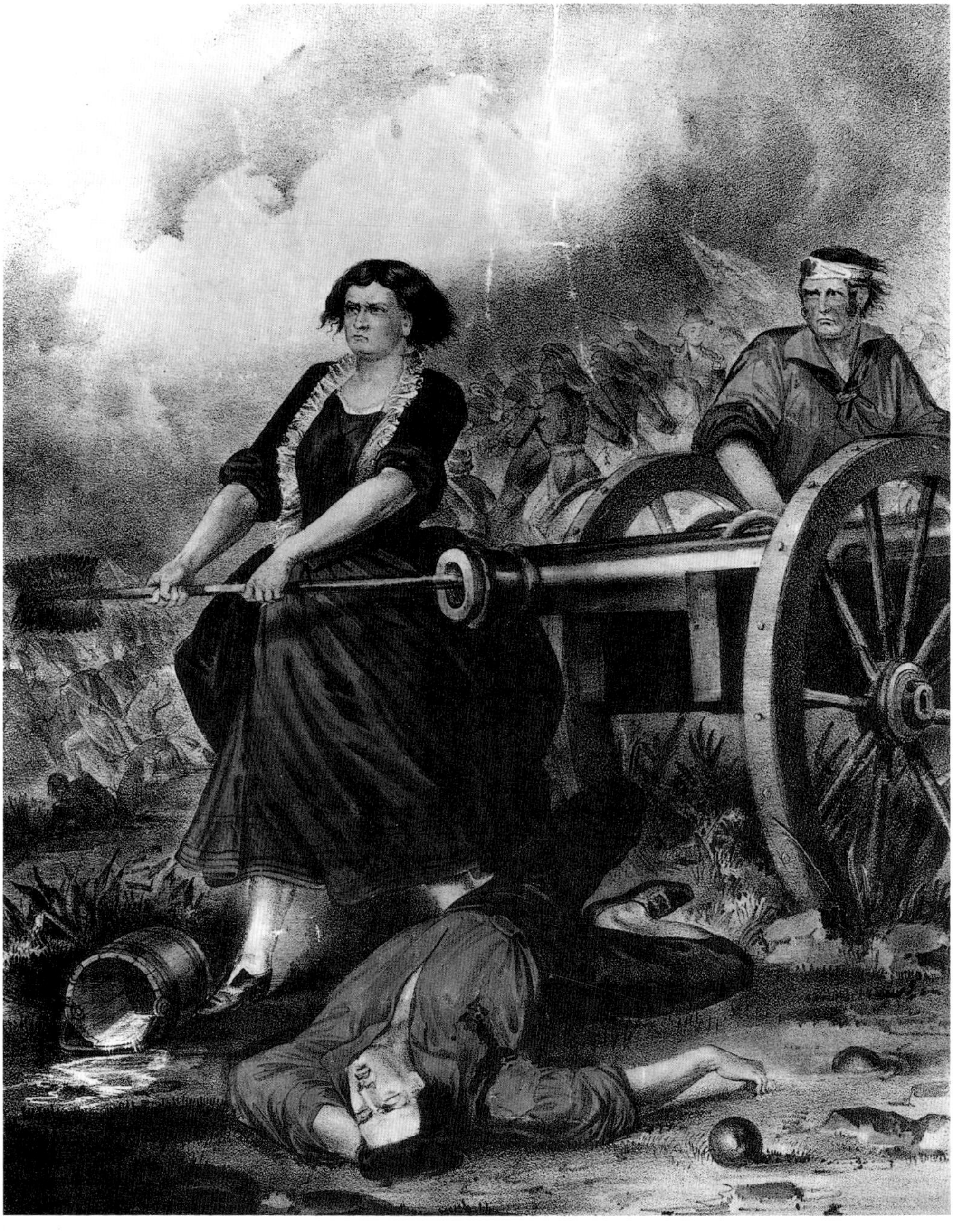

June

S	M	T	W	T	F	S
1	2	3	4	5	6	7
8	9	10	11	12	13	14
15	16	17	18	19	20	21
22	23	24	25	26	27	28
29	30					

"MOLLY PITCHER" (MARY HAYS McCAULEY)
(1754–1832)
Revolutionary heroine

Women's contributions to the American Revolution, though largely unsung, ranged from running the family farm to enduring the heat of battle.

In 1769, "Molly" Ludwig married John Caspar Hays, who served in the First and Seventh Pennsylvania Regiments. On June 28, 1778, the day of the Battle of Monmouth, she was on the field with him. Throughout the blazing afternoon, she brought water to the exhausted soldiers, thereby earning the nickname "Molly Pitcher." Later, when her husband collapsed from the heat, Molly took over at his cannon, serving in his stead for the remainder of the battle.

In 1822 the General Assembly of Pennsylvania passed "An act for the relief of Molly M'Kolly" in honor of her services, providing her an annuity and a cash grant of forty dollars. Monuments were erected at her grave in 1876 and 1916. Her likeness also appears on the monument commemorating the Battle of Monmouth.

Prints and Photographs Division

Russian poet Anna Akhmatove b. 1889

23 Monday — 174

American novelist Rebecca Blaine Harding Davis, mother and fiercest critic of journalist and novelist Richard Harding Davis, b. 1831

24 Tuesday — 175

Carly Simon, singer and composer, b. 1945

25 Wednesday — 176

Pearl Buck, winner of the 1938 Nobel Prize in literature, b. 1892

26 Thursday — 177

Antoinette Perry, founder of the American Theater Wing and namesake of the Tony Awards, b. 1888

Last Quarter

27 Friday — 178

Molly Pitcher takes the place of her wounded husband in the Battle of Monmouth, 1778

28 Saturday — 179

Journalist and writer Oriana Fallaci b. 1930

29 Sunday — 180

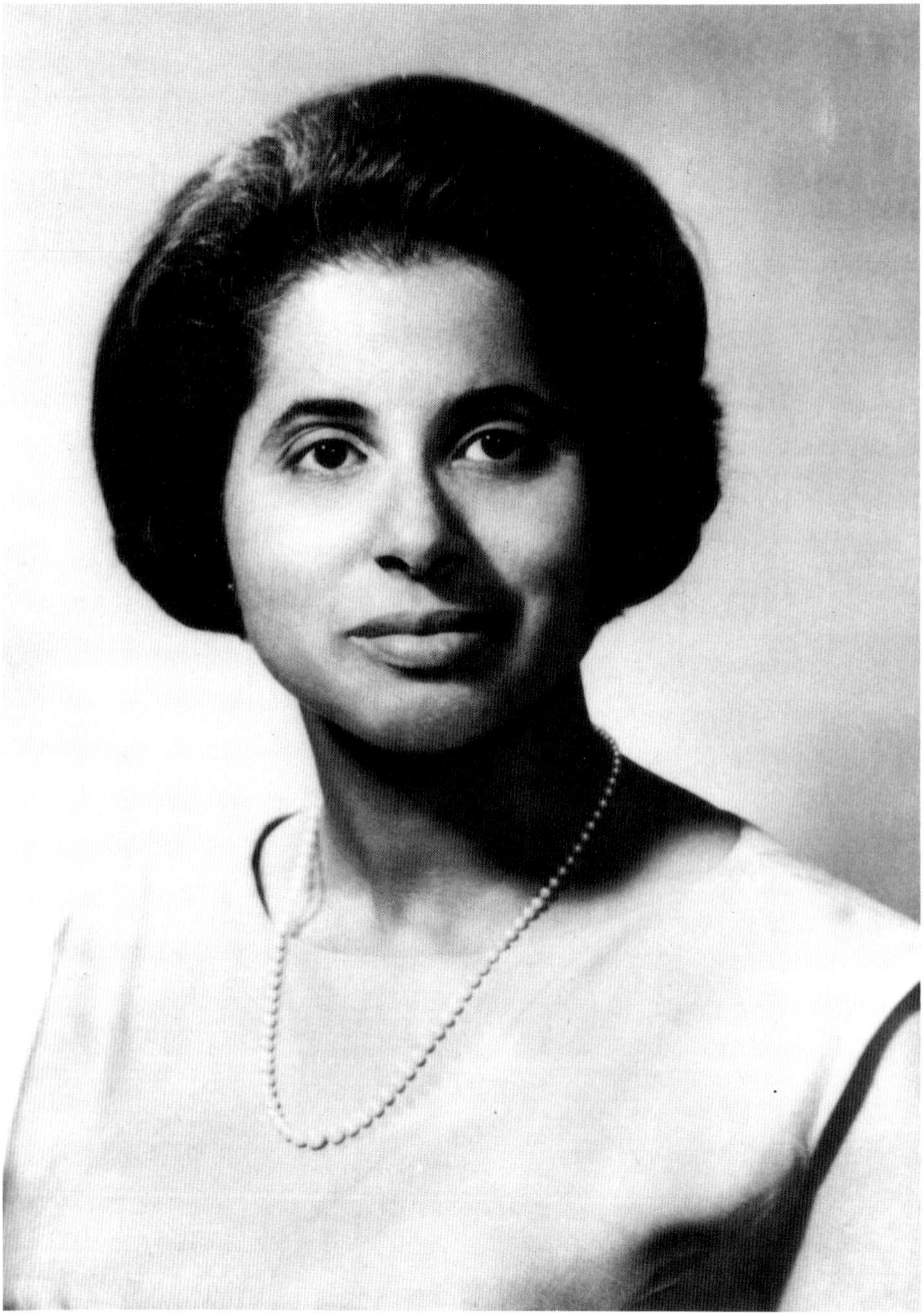

Jun/Jul

JULY

S	M	T	W	T	F	S
		1	2	3	4	5
6	7	8	9	10	11	12
13	14	15	16	17	18	19
20	21	22	23	24	25	26
27	28	29	30	31		

PATRICIA ROBERTS HARRIS
(1924–1985)
Lawyer, public official

From her early academic achievements to her pathbreaking legal and political career, Patricia Roberts Harris exploded stereotypes. Born in rural Matoon, Illinois, Roberts graduated from high school with scholarship offers from five colleges. She chose Howard University, where she graduated in 1945 summa cum laude, and was also vice-chair of the student NAACP chapter and a sit-in participant in segregated Washington, D.C. A lifelong activist in promoting equal rights for blacks and women, Harris worked as a teacher and administrator at Howard while taking part in a range of civil rights and social welfare commissions. In 1965 Lyndon Johnson appointed her ambassador to Luxembourg, making her the first African American woman to head a U.S. embassy. When Jimmy Carter tapped her to head the Department of Housing and Urban Development, she became the first African American woman to hold a cabinet post; she also served later as secretary of health, education, and welfare (now health and human services).

Patricia Roberts Harris Collection
Manuscript Division

Entertainer Lena Horne b. 1917

30 Monday

Choreographer Twyla Tharp b. 1942

Canada Day (Canada)

1 Tuesday

Amelia Earhart loses radio contact over the Pacific, 1937

2 Wednesday

Maria Martin, the only woman among naturalist James Audubon's three assistants, b. 1796

3 Thursday

Mary H. Myers becomes the first woman to ascend in a balloon (in the first of many flights over 40 years), 1880

Independence Day
New Moon

4 Friday

Juanita M. Kreps becomes the first female governor of the New York Stock Exchange, 1972

5 Saturday

English children's writer and illustrator Beatrix Potter b. 1866

6 Sunday

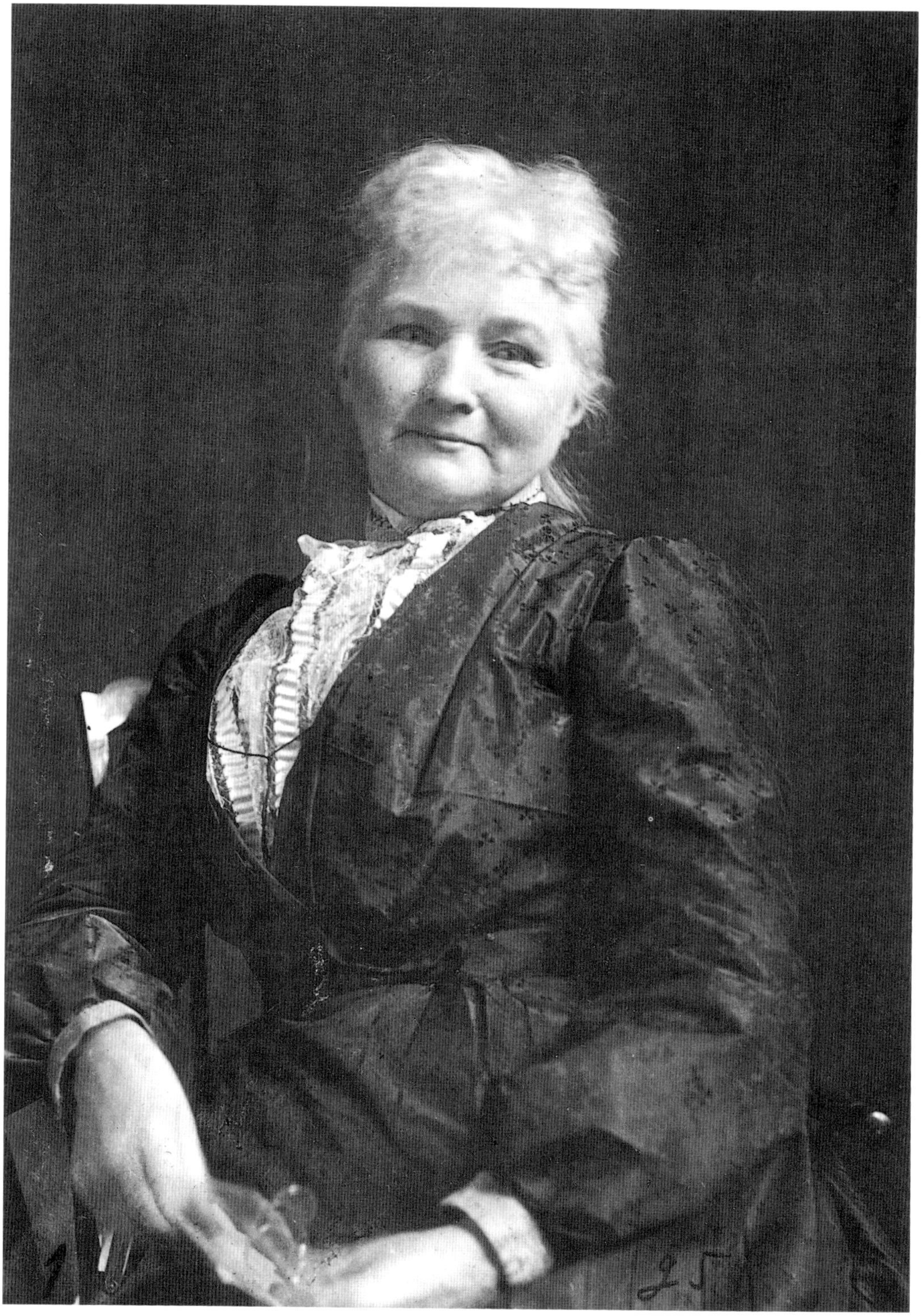

July

S	M	T	W	T	F	S
		1	2	3	4	5
6	7	8	9	10	11	12
13	14	15	16	17	18	19
20	21	22	23	24	25	26
27	28	29	30	31		

MARY HARRIS "MOTHER" JONES
(1830–1930)
Labor organizer

Mother Jones was one of the most fiery and individualistic figures in the American labor movement. A native of Cork, Ireland, she emigrated to the United States as a child. After losing her husband and children to yellow fever in 1867, and her dressmaking business to the Chicago fire in 1871, Jones became a full-time labor organizer. Her motto was "Pray for the dead and fight like hell for the living."

The labor movement itself became her home; as she put it, "My address is like my shoes. It travels with me. I abide where there is a fight against wrong." She was one of the founders of the Industrial Workers of the World, and she worked throughout the United States to organize miners, garment workers, and steelworkers. An ardent child labor abolitionist as well, she led a march of child textile workers in 1903 to President Theodore Roosevelt's home.

Outspoken and unafraid of conflict, Mother Jones worked all her life on behalf of working people and was saluted by admirers and adversaries alike on her hundredth birthday.

Prints and Photographs Division

Martina Navratilova wins her third straight Wimbledon singles crown, 1984

7 Monday — 188

Artist Käthe Kollwitz b. 1867

8 Tuesday — 189

Poet June Jordan b. 1936

9 Wednesday — 190

First meeting of the National Women's Political Caucus is held, 1971

10 Thursday — 191

Susan Warner, author of *The Wide, Wide World,* the first novel to sell one million copies in the U.S., b. 1819

11 Friday — 192

Norwegian soprano Kirsten Flagstad b. 1895

First Quarter

12 Saturday — 193

Pilot Cora Sterling becomes the first female aerial police officer in Seattle, Wash., 1934

13 Sunday — 194

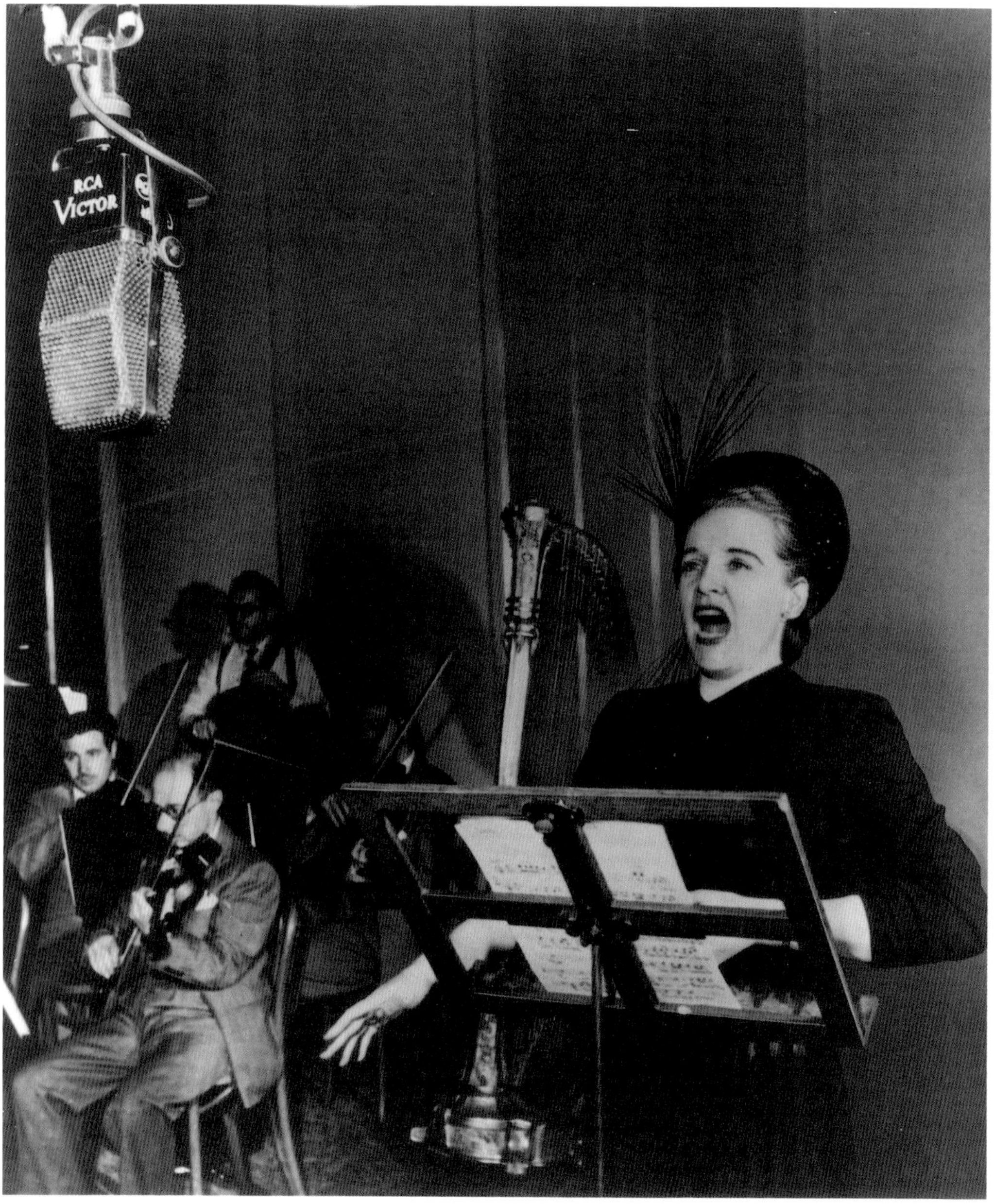
RCA
VICTOR

July

S	M	T	W	T	F	S
		1	2	3	4	5
6	7	8	9	10	11	12
13	14	15	16	17	18	19
20	21	22	23	24	25	26
27	28	29	30	31		

ELEANOR STEBER
(1914–1990)
Opera singer, teacher

Best remembered for her peerless interpretations of Mozart, Eleanor Steber was a leading singer of the Metropolitan Opera from 1940, when she won the Met's radio auditions, until 1966, when she retired from the operatic stage to teach full-time. Considered by many to be the most important American soprano between Rosa Ponselle and Leontyne Price, Steber was also the only soprano of her time whose extensive repertoire encompassed French, Italian, and German opera equally. Her recordings numbered more than one hundred (the photograph here shows her in a session in the late 1940s), and for several years she operated her own label, St/And Records. It was also Steber who commissioned Samuel Barber's song cycle, "Knoxville, Summer of 1916." Long associated with the voice faculties of the Cleveland Institute, Juilliard, and CUNY/Brooklyn, in 1975 she established the Eleanor Steber Foundation to help younger singers.

RCA Victor Records Photograph
Prints and Photographs Division

Author, mountaineer, and archaeologist Gertrude Bell b. 1868

14 Monday — 195

Novelist Iris Murdoch *(A Severed Head)* b. 1919

15 Tuesday — 196

Journalist and antilynching crusader Ida B. Wells-Barnett b. 1862

16 Wednesday — 197

Eleanor Steber, opera singer, b. 1914

17 Thursday — 198

Geraldine A. Ferraro is nominated for the office of vice president of the U.S., 1984

18 Friday — 199

"We hold these truths to be self-evident: that all men and women are created equal. . . ." Declaration of Sentiments is adopted at the first U.S. women's rights convention, Seneca Falls, N.Y., 1848

19 Saturday — 200

U.S. senator Barbara Mikulski b. 1936

Full Moon

20 Sunday — 201

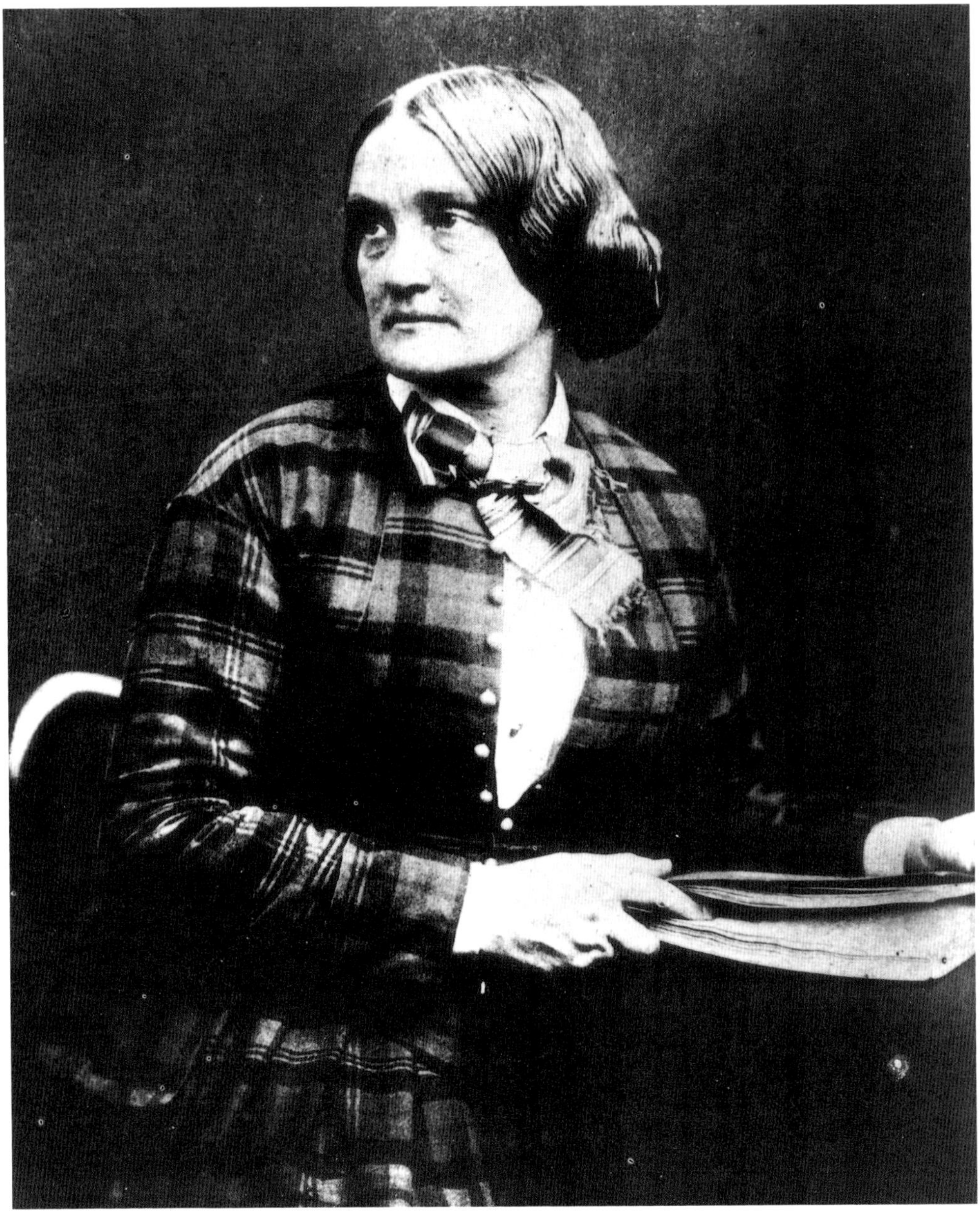

July

S	M	T	W	T	F	S
		1	2	3	4	5
6	7	8	9	10	11	12
13	14	15	16	17	18	19
20	21	22	23	24	25	26
27	28	29	30	31		

CHARLOTTE CUSHMAN
(1816–1876)
Actor

Charlotte Cushman was recognized as the foremost female American actor of the nineteenth century, and she is one of the great artists and personalities whose legacy remains yet to be fully appreciated. Born in Massachusetts, Cushman trained for the operatic stage after her father's death left her without means. She found the dramatic stage more suited to her talents, however, and made her debut as Lady Macbeth at age nineteen. Thereafter she acted with companies in New York and gained her first significant acclaim. Between 1845 and 1849 she acted in London, playing both female and male roles; her Romeo, according to one critic, was "real, palpably real . . . my blood ran hot and cold." Having honed her art and gained widespread fame, she toured the United States for several years, then "retired" any number of times. In one of her most famous roles, that of Queen Katherine, Cushman caused author William Winter to shrink back to the rear of his box from the blaze of her eyes; of Cushman in another signature role, Meg Merrilies, he wrote: "Her voice . . . had in it an unearthly music that made the nerves thrill and the brain tremble."

Photograph courtesy Vincent Virga

Louise Bethune, first female American architect, b. 1856

21 Monday — 202

Author and etiquette authority Amy Vanderbilt b. 1908

22 Tuesday — 203

Actor Charlotte Cushman b. 1816

23 Wednesday — 204

Wildlife biologist and elephant researcher Cynthia Moss b. 1940

24 Thursday — 205

Annette Abbott Adams is sworn in as the first female district attorney of the U.S. (Northern California District), 1918

25 Friday — 206

Burmese human rights leader Aung San Suu Kyi is placed under house arrest, 1989

Last Quarter

26 Saturday — 207

Skater and Olympic gold medalist Dorothy Hamill b. 1956

27 Sunday — 208

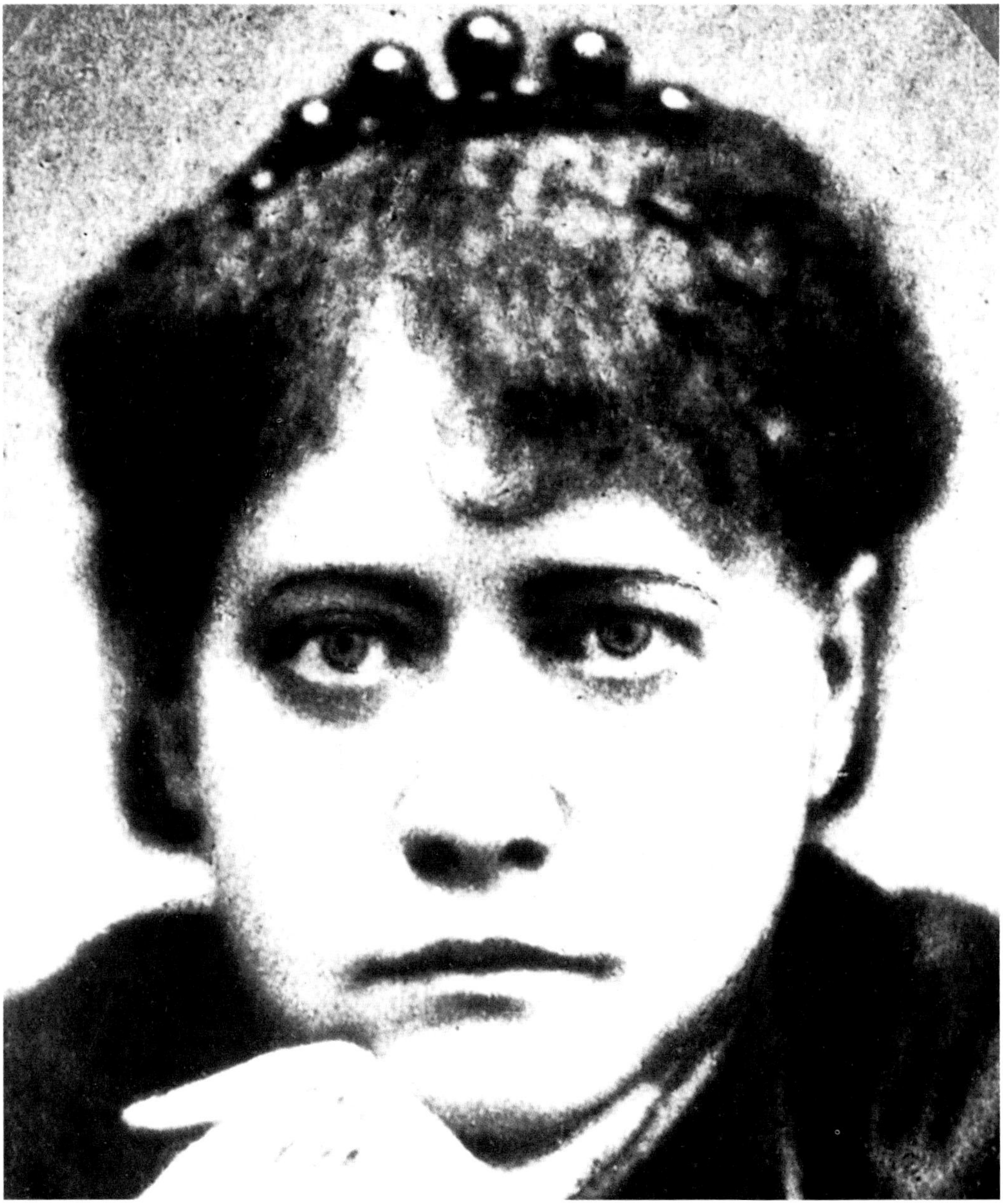

Jul/Aug

AUGUST						
S	M	T	W	T	F	S
					1	2
3	4	5	6	7	8	9
10	11	12	13	14	15	16
17	18	19	20	21	22	23
24	25	26	27	28	29	30
31						

HELENA BLAVATSKY
(1831–1891)
Spiritual leader, author

Helena Blavatsky was an early traveler on roads that would be trod in the twentieth century by Carl Jung, Joseph Campbell, Elisabeth Kübler-Ross, Niels Bohr, Gaia theorist Lynn Margulis, and the current Dalai Lama—to name but a handful of modern explorers of the realms where consciousness, physical phenomena, and the laws of nature converge. A native of Ukraine, Blavatsky is best remembered as a principal founder of the Theosophical Society (est. 1875) and developer of "theosophy"—so called after the Greek words *theos* (divinity) and *sophia* (wisdom). Nonsectarian and based on tenets of universal community, the essential unity of all knowledge, and the interdependence of all phenomena, theosophy is also concerned with extrasensory and other untapped human powers. For this reason it tended to be seen as yet another variety of nineteenth-century quack spiritualism. Yet Blavatsky, in works such as *Isis Unveiled* (1877), proved far-seeing in her holistic treatment of topics such as gnosticism, Eastern cosmology, and Platonic philosophy.

Prints and Photographs Division

Elizabeth Ellery Bailey is confirmed as the first female member of the Civil Aeronautics Board, 1977

209
28
Monday

Volleyball legend Flo Hyman b. 1954

210
29
Tuesday

Emma Gillett, cofounder of Washington College of Law, b. 1852

211
30
Wednesday

Russian theosophist and traveler Helena Blavatsky b. 1831

212
31
Thursday

Harriet Quimby becomes the first licensed female pilot in the U.S., 1911

213
1
Friday

Actor Myrna Loy b. 1905

214
2
Saturday

Mystery novelist P. D. (Phyllis Dorothy) James b. 1920

New Moon

215
3
Sunday

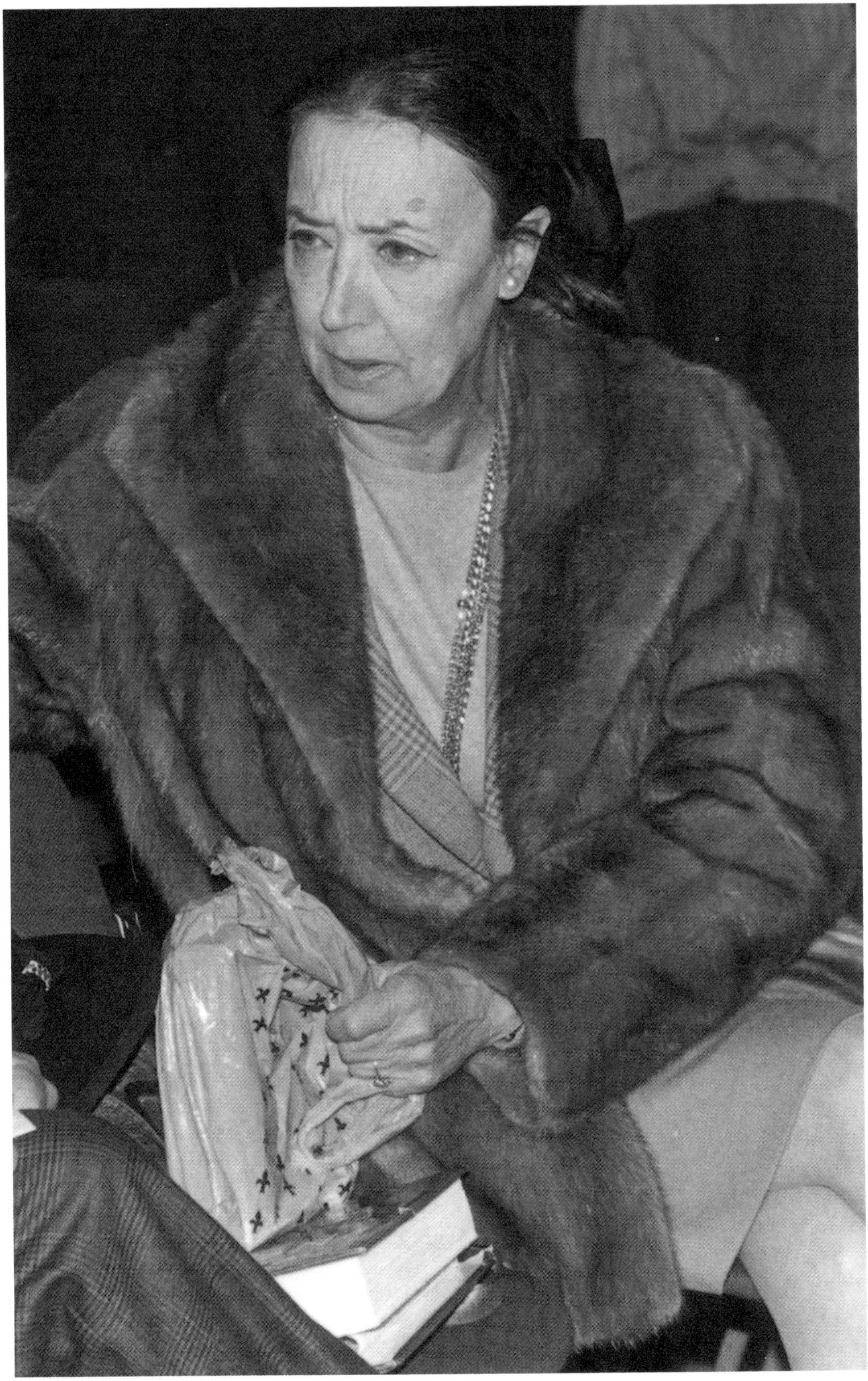

August

S	M	T	W	T	F	S
					1	2
3	4	5	6	7	8	9
10	11	12	13	14	15	16
17	18	19	20	21	22	23
24	25	26	27	28	29	30
31						

ORIANA FALLACI
(b. 1930)
Journalist, author

Widely regarded as one of the most powerful and provocative interviewers of our time, Oriana Fallaci has also made her mark as a war correspondent, novelist, and social critic whose fiercely independent thought resists easy categorization.
    Born in Florence, Italy, to a family steeped in poverty and anti-Fascist resistance, Fallaci would later describe her early life as "very, very tough" and "full of grief." During World War II she served as a courier for the resistance and as a guide for downed Allied pilots. After the war Fallaci entered medical school, working part-time as a reporter to help finance her education.
    Journalism proved to be her calling, and she worked her way from the crime beat of a Florentine daily to special correspondent for *Europeo,* a prominent Italian weekly. For some two decades thereafter Fallaci forged an international reputation both as a journalist (her series on the Vietnam War won the Italian equivalent of the Pulitzer Prize) and as a unique political interviewer, revealing unseen sides of subjects from Henry Kissinger to the Ayatollah Khomeini.

Photo by Yusef El-Amin
Library of Congress

Susanna Wright, Pennsylvania frontierswoman who served as scribe, arbiter, and physician to the Conestoga Indians, b. 1697

4 Monday — 216

Historian Mary Ritter Beard *(Woman as a Force in History)* b. 1876

5 Tuesday — 217

Queen Wilhelmina of the Netherlands becomes the first reigning queen to address a joint session of the U.S. Congress, 1941

6 Wednesday — 218

Mata Hari b. 1876

7 Thursday — 219

Marjorie Kinnan Rawlings, winner of the 1939 Pulitzer Prize for *The Yearling,* b. 1896

8 Friday — 220

Singer Whitney Houston b. 1963

9 Saturday — 221

Anna J. Cooper, black educator and president of Frelinghuysen University, b. 1859

10 Sunday — 222

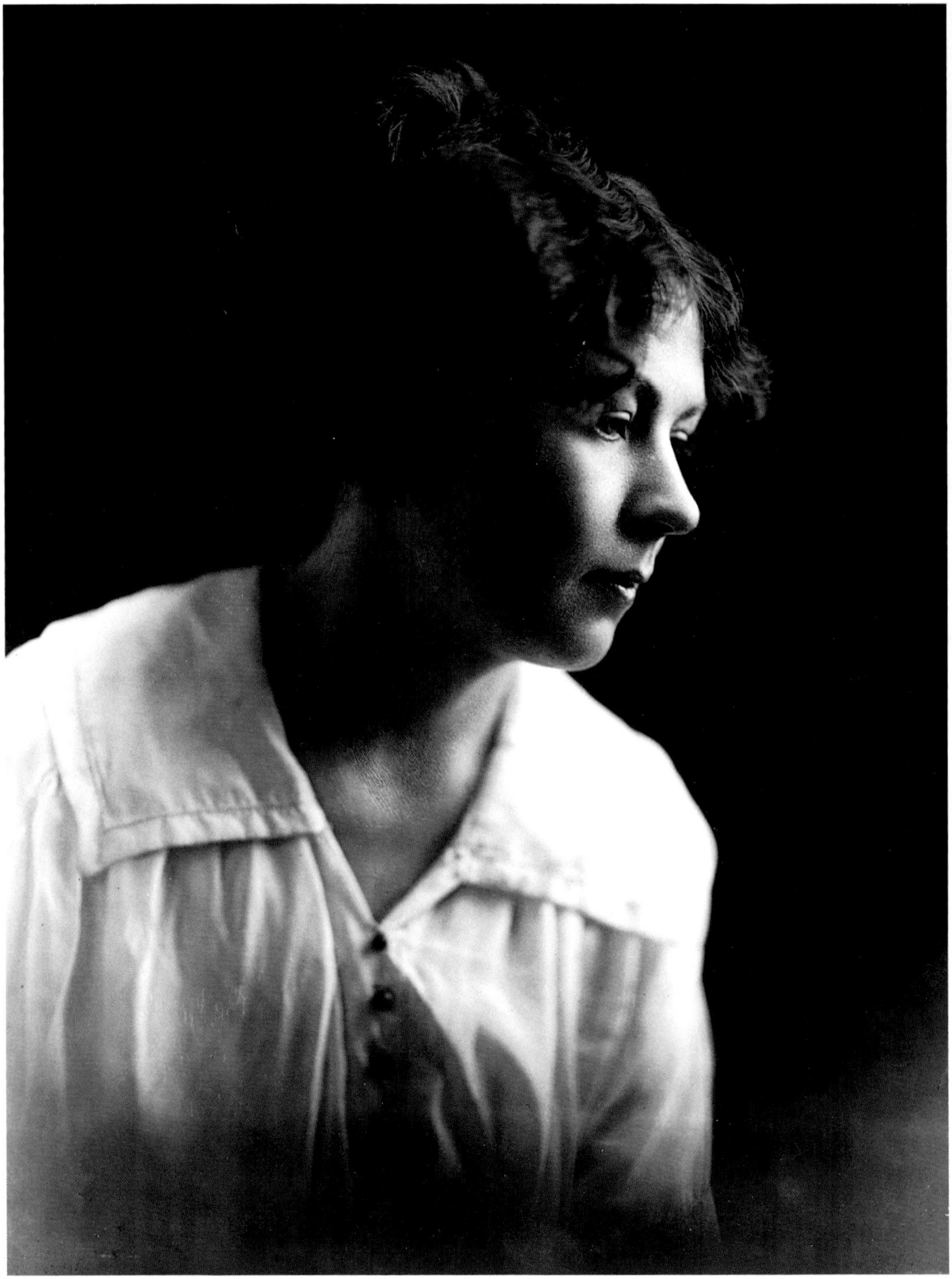

August

S	M	T	W	T	F	S
					1	2
3	4	5	6	7	8	9
10	11	12	13	14	15	16
17	18	19	20	21	22	23
24	25	26	27	28	29	30
31

CHRISTABEL PANKHURST
(1880–1958)
Suffragist, reformer

Songwriter Nancy White's wry "Daughters of Feminists" laments the tendency of younger women to be oblivious of the struggles of their elders. But in families such as that of Lucy Stone, Elizabeth Cady Stanton, and the Pankhursts of England, such was hardly the case. All three children of militant suffragist Emmeline Pankhurst—Christabel, Sylvia, and Adela—became activists for women's rights and other reformist causes. The precocious and keenly analytical Christabel Pankhurst, coming upon a scene in which forty years of suffrage agitation had barely made a dent in public opinion, devised a plan of action by which the government, rather than suffragists, would be repeatedly put on the defensive, while increasing the movement's visibility. The campaign proved both tumultuous and highly effective, though Pankhurst had to direct it from exile in Paris between 1912 and 1914. In later years this complex reformer channeled her energies into evangelical Christianity as a preacher and speaker. She was created a Dame Commander of the British Empire in 1936.
Prints and Photographs Division

Sarah Bernhardt makes her stage debut in *Iphigenie*, Paris, 1862

First Quarter

11 Monday — 223

Katharine Lee Bates, poet and author of "America the Beautiful," b. 1859

12 Tuesday — 224

Abolitionist and suffragist Lucy Stone b. 1818

13 Wednesday — 225

Jockey Robyn Smith b. 1944

14 Thursday — 226

Author and broadcaster Linda Ellerbee b. 1944

15 Friday — 227

Author Margaret Mitchell, age 48, dies after being hit by a drunk driver, 1949

16 Saturday — 228

Laura de Force Gordon, newspaperwoman and pioneering California suffragist, b. 1838

17 Sunday — 229

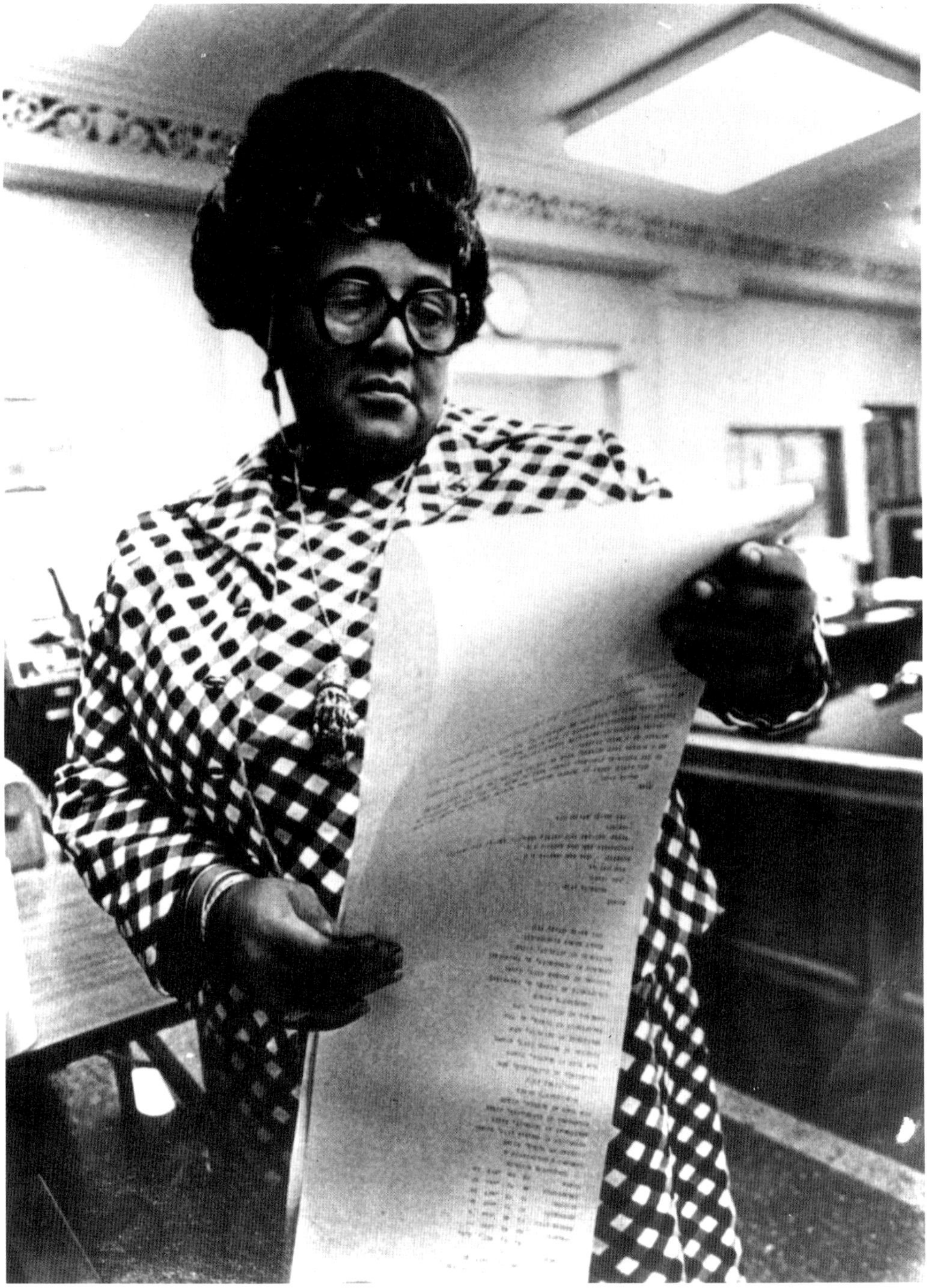

August

S	M	T	W	T	F	S
					1	2
3	4	5	6	7	8	9
10	11	12	13	14	15	16
17	18	19	20	21	22	23
24	25	26	27	28	29	30
31						

ETHEL L. PAYNE
(1911–1991)
Journalist

Known as the "First Lady of the Black Press," Ethel Payne got her start in journalism in 1951 when she was hired as a reporter by the *Chicago Defender*. Establishing a reputation for solid writing and straightforward observations, Payne moved to Washington, D.C., and covered the nascent civil rights movement for the *Defender*. One of the first black women accredited to the White House Press Corps, Payne, in the words of one colleague, "asked the questions we should have been asking"—on one occasion pressing President Eisenhower so persistently about his plans for desegregating interstate travel that the confrontation became a front-page story. Payne's years of civil rights coverage earned her an invitation to the Oval Office to witness President Johnson's signing of the Civil Rights Act of 1964. In the mid-1960s, she turned to international affairs, eventually covering thirty countries on six continents. In 1972, she became the first black female commentator employed by a national broadcast network when she was hired by CBS.

Ethel L. Payne Collection
Manuscript Division

---

18 Monday — 230
Tennessee becomes the 36th and final state to ratify the 19th Amendment (woman suffrage), 1920
Full Moon

19 Tuesday — 231
Prison reformer Mary Belle Harris b. 1874

20 Wednesday — 232
The Abbey Theatre is founded in Dublin by Lady Gregory and William Butler Yeats, 1904

21 Thursday — 233
Composer Lili Boulanger b. 1893

22 Friday — 234
Katherine Anne Porter embarks on the same voyage—from Veracruz, Mexico, to Bremerhaven, Germany—that will serve as the setting for her 1962 novel *Ship of Fools*, 1931

23 Saturday — 235
Sarah Whiting, physicist and astronomer, b. 1847

24 Sunday — 236
Nature writer and mystic Margaret Fairless Barber ("Michael Fairless") dies in England at age 32 after a long illness, 1901

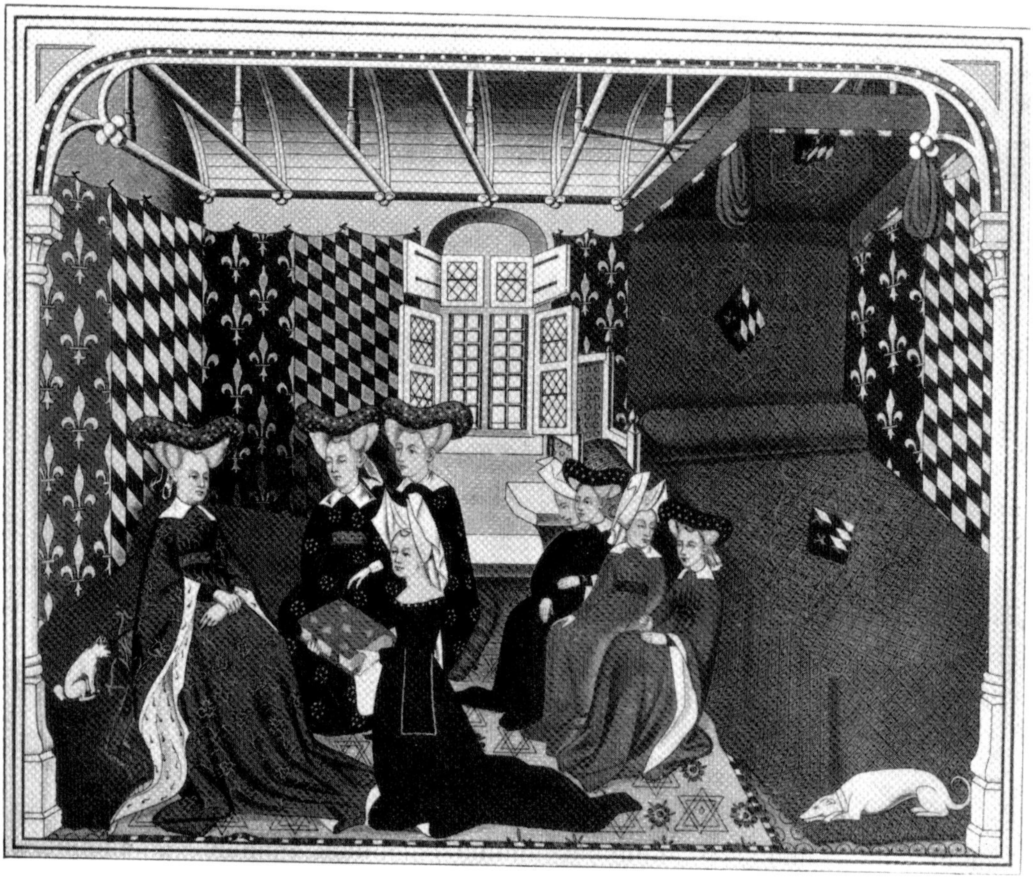

August

S	M	T	W	T	F	S
					1	2
3	4	5	6	7	8	9
10	11	12	13	14	15	16
17	18	19	20	21	22	23
24	25	26	27	28	29	30
31						

CHRISTINE DE PISAN
(ca. 1364–1430)
Writer, feminist

Raised in the exclusive world of the French court, Christine de Pisan studied liberal arts under the guidance of her father, who encouraged her curiosity despite her mother's—and society's—disapproval of education for girls. Her privileged and happy life was clouded at age twenty-five, when the deaths of her father and husband forced her to find a way to support herself and her family. Beginning work as a manuscript copyist, she went on to become the first woman known to make a living as a writer. An original thinker and a writer facile in lyric poetry as well as didactic writing, de Pisan challenged public opinion and was an outspoken feminist. She argued against the theory of women's inferiority and against the misogyny so prevalent in the work of her male counterparts. An astute political pundit as well, de Pisan predicted in 1405 the French downfall at Agincourt ten years later. Her final poem was an account of the triumphant Joan of Arc, who freed Orleans and conducted Charles VII of France to his coronation.
General Collections

Malvina Reynolds, singer, composer, and activist, b. 1900

Last Quarter

237
25
Monday

The 19th Amendment formally takes effect: "The right of citizens of the United States to vote shall not be denied or abridged . . . on account of sex," 1920

238
26
Tuesday

Sophia Smith, founder of Smith College, b. 1910

239
27
Wednesday

Rita Dove, author, educator, and U.S. Poet Laureate, b. 1952

240
28
Thursday

Singer Dinah Washington b. 1924

241
29
Friday

Frankenstein author Mary Wollstonecraft Shelley b. 1797

242
30
Saturday

Educator Maria Montessori b. 1870

243
31
Sunday

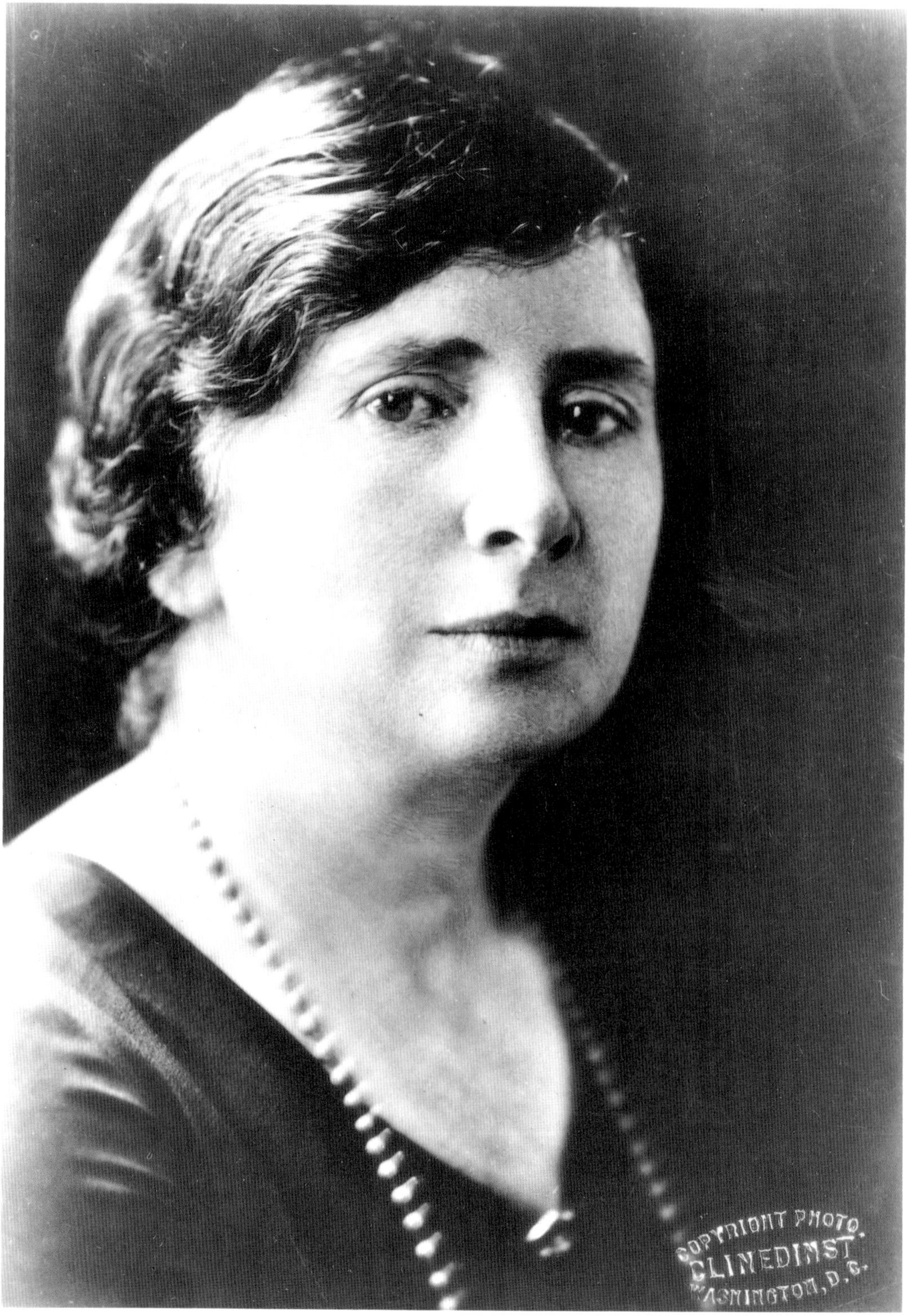
COPYRIGHT PHOTO.
CLINEDINST
WASHINGTON, D.C.

September

S	M	T	W	T	F	S
	1	2	3	4	5	6
7	8	9	10	11	12	13
14	15	16	17	18	19	20
21	22	23	24	25	26	27
28	29	30				

ROSE SCHNEIDERMAN
(1882–1972)
Union organizer

As a key figure in the National Women's Trade Union League (WTUL), Rose Schneiderman operated in a realm where class issues—laid bare by the fledgling labor movement—intersected with those of gender. With drive and adroit leadership, Schneiderman built the collective strength of urban working women by fostering a sense of economic sisterhood among them in the years before suffrage was won (she also garnered crucial support for suffrage among male workers). Thereafter she fought for both female opportunity and trade unionism—believing firmly in the latter as a means to the former—while fighting for such reforms as the eight-hour day and the minimum wage. Schneiderman also pioneered social and educational programs for working women, and during the years she served as national president of the WTUL she was an effective communicator of labor concerns to the government and media. She was also the only woman on the advisory board of Franklin Roosevelt's National Recovery Administration.

Prints and Photographs Division

244
Naturalist Anna Botsford Comstock b. 1854

Labor Day (U.S. and Canada)
New Moon

1
Monday

245
Christa McAuliffe, first teacher in space, b. 1948

2
Tuesday

246
Texas politician and governor Ann Richards b. 1933

3
Wednesday

247
Katherine Biddle, popular U.S. poet of the 1920s, b. 1902

4
Thursday

248
Pianist and composer Amy Beach b. 1867

5
Friday

249
Jane Addams b. 1860

6
Saturday

250
English novelist Taylor Caldwell b. 1900

7
Sunday

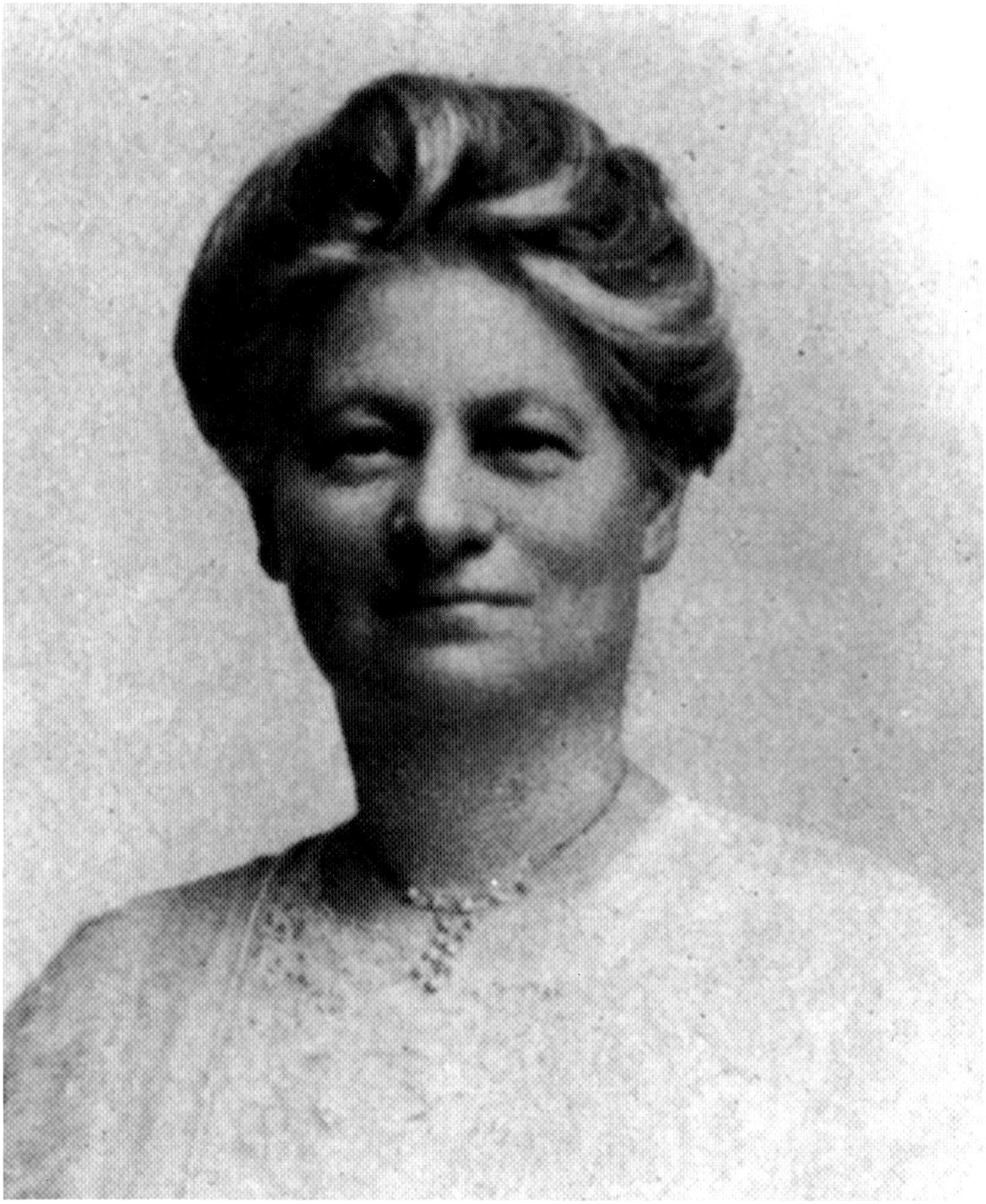

September

S	M	T	W	T	F	S
	1	2	3	4	5	6
7	8	9	10	11	12	13
14	15	16	17	18	19	20
21	22	23	24	25	26	27
28	29	30				

HANNAH GREENEBAUM SOLOMON (1858–1942)
Reformer, clubwoman

Resplendent in white lace and shielded by a fashionable parasol, Hannah Greenebaum Solomon, as chair of a committee that was investigating Chicago's waste disposal system, tromped through the city's dumps on an inspection tour in 1910. While she later used the image to illustrate the quixotic spirit and lack of preparedness of herself and others in fighting society's ills, the image is also emblematic of the determination of many educated women at the turn of the century to reform aspects of society from labor laws to sanitation systems. Solomon herself helped to establish Chicago's Cook County juvenile court system and was active in other areas as well. The daughter of German Jewish immigrants, Solomon had a special concern for the plight of fellow immigrants in Chicago in the 1890s; to serve them effectively, she established an organization that helped and gave legal advice to the immigrants. She also sought to expand women's networking and visibility across a range of political and social realms; this led to her founding of the National Council of Jewish Women and several other clubs.

General Collections

251
Hani Mokoto, Japanese journalist and educator, b. 1873

8
Monday

252
Author Phyllis Whitney b. 1903

9
Tuesday

253
Women's Auxiliary Ferrying Squadron (WAFS) established, 1942

First Quarter

10
Wednesday

254
Rosika Schwimmer, pacifist and internationalist, b. 1877

11
Thursday

255
Actor Margaret Hamilton, dean of cinematic wicked witches, b. 1902

12
Friday

256
Author Judith Martin (a.k.a. Miss Manners) b. 1938

13
Saturday

257
Birth control advocate Margaret Sanger b. 1879

14
Sunday

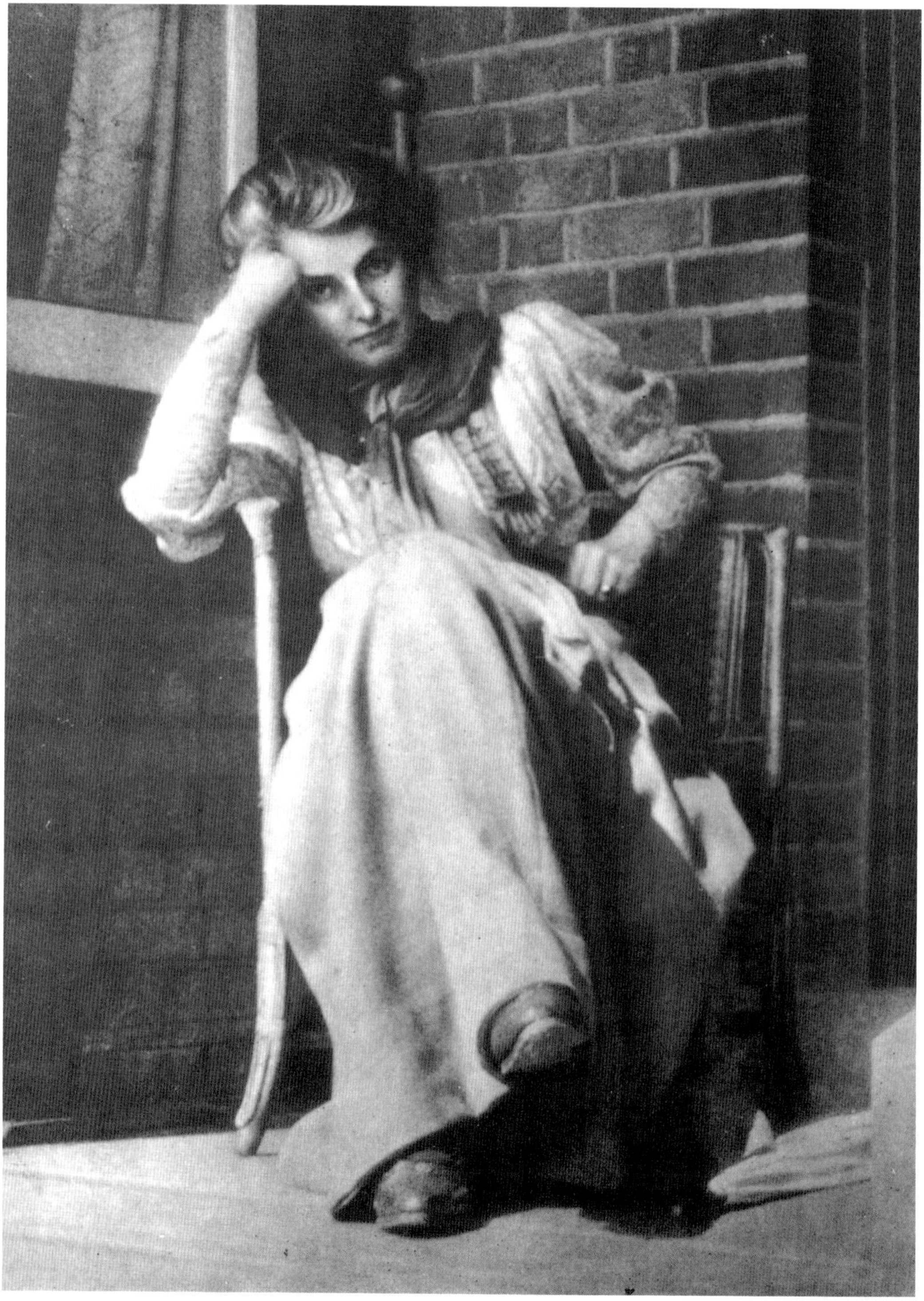

September

S	M	T	W	T	F	S
	1	2	3	4	5	6
7	8	9	10	11	12	13
14	15	16	17	18	19	20
21	22	23	24	25	26	27
28	29	30				

BEATRICE WEBB
(1858–1943)
Economist, reformer

Born to a life of *nouveau-riche* comfort as the daughter of a railroad promoter, Beatrice Webb came to be one of the best-known figures in British reformist politics in the early twentieth century. With her husband, Sidney, Webb spearheaded a critique of industrial society whose legacies are many and to which the Webbs' personal contributions include the first minimum wage laws, development of the Labour Party, and founding of the London School of Economics.
  Like Jane Addams and others of her generation, Beatrice Webb found her calling—and her freedom—in social work, documenting and addressing the vast unmet needs of the urban poor. After being drawn to the Fabian Society, a group (named for a Roman exemplifier of patience) dedicated to socialist ideals and gradualist politics, Webb and her husband became its pillars, authoring or coauthoring more than 100 works, including the monumental *Industrial Democracy* (1897). This photograph was taken by a Fabian colleague and friend, George Bernard Shaw.
General Collections

Louise B. Bethune becomes the first female architect elected to the American Institute of Architects, 1890

258
15
Monday

Ella Crandall, pioneer of visiting-nurse programs, b. 1871

Full Moon

259
16
Tuesday

Maureen Connelly, first woman to win a "grand slam" in tennis, b. 1934

260
17
Wednesday

Religious rebel Anne Hutchinson arrives in Boston from England, 1634

261
18
Thursday

Pop singer "Mama" Cass Elliott b. 1941

262
19
Friday

Billie Jean King beats Bobby Riggs in the "Battle of the Sexes" tennis match, Houston, 1973

263
20
Saturday

Playwright Marsha Norman b. 1947

264
21
Sunday

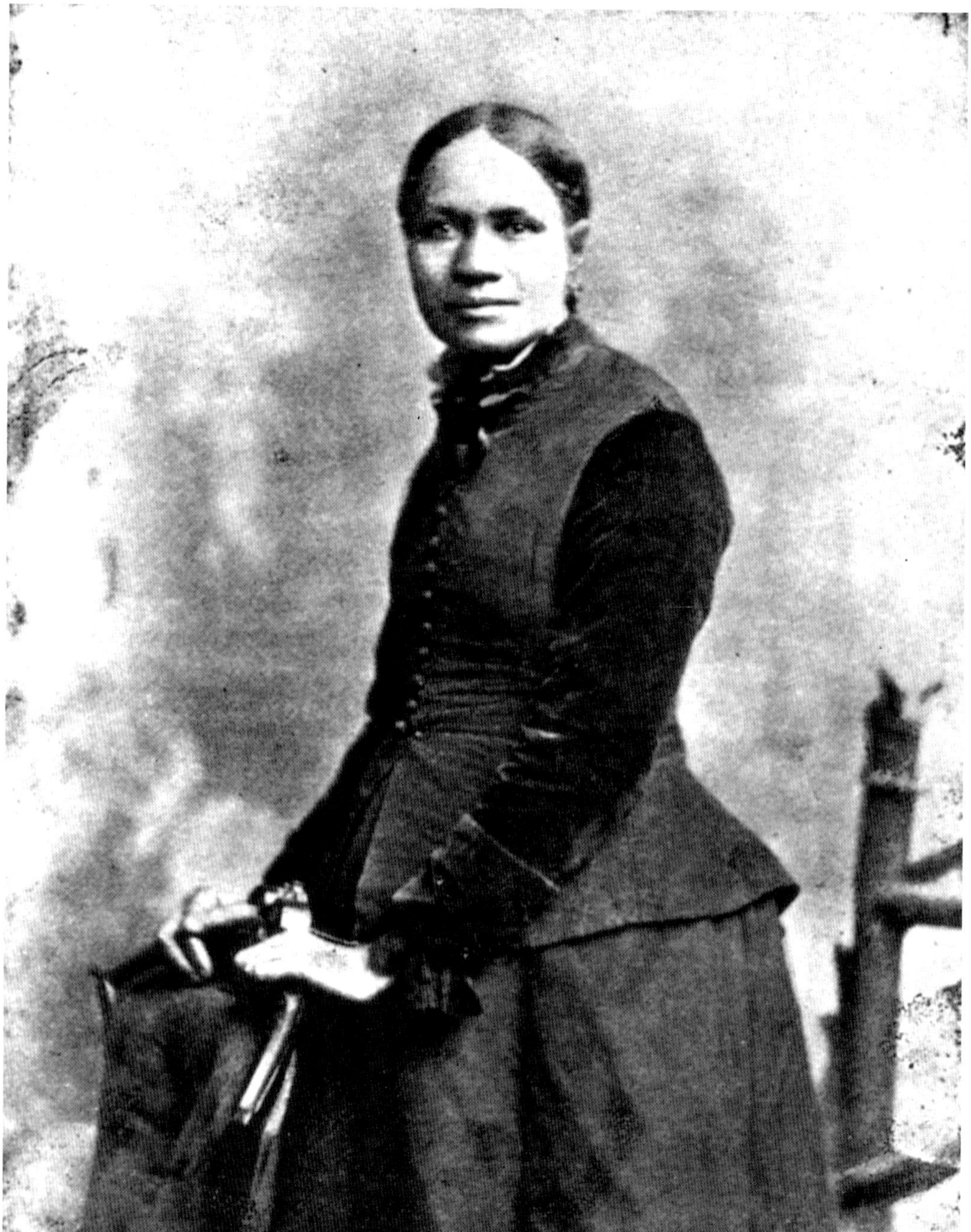

September

S	M	T	W	T	F	S
	1	2	3	4	5	6
7	8	9	10	11	12	13
14	15	16	17	18	19	20
21	22	23	24	25	26	27
28	29	30				

FRANCES E. W. HARPER
(1825–1911)
Abolitionist, feminist, poet

The most prominent African American poet to appear after Phillis Wheatley, Frances E. W. Harper was born of free blacks in Maryland (then a slave state) and raised by an aunt and uncle who ran a school. After she began working, in her teens, she had the good fortune to have her love of reading and learning nurtured by her employer, who owned a bookstore and encouraged her reading. As she grew up and watched slave laws became more rather than less repressive, Harper began to speak and write about the cruelty and inhumanity of slavery. Leaving Maryland in 1850, she taught at Union Seminary in Ohio and began a lecturing career in 1854 with the address "Education and the Elevation of the Colored Race." From 1856 to 1860, she spoke for the Anti-Slavery Society in Maine, and after emancipation she continued to tour and speak on behalf of equal rights for the newly freed slaves. A feminist, Harper founded the National Association of Colored Women. Her many poems and her novel *Iola Leroy* are charged with emotion and serve as snapshots of the South during reconstruction.

General Collections

Judge Sandra Day O'Connor's nomination to the U.S. Supreme Court is confirmed, 1981

Autumnal Equinox 11:56 P.M. (GMT)

22 Monday — 265

Antinuclear activist Mary Sinclair b. 1918

Last Quarter

23 Tuesday — 266

Poet and activist Frances E. W. Harper b. 1825

24 Wednesday — 267

Broadcast journalist Barbara Walters b. 1931

25 Thursday — 268

Country music star Lynn Anderson b. 1947

26 Friday — 269

Sarah De Crow, first female U.S. postmaster, b. 1792

27 Saturday — 270

Blues singer Koko Taylor b. 1935

28 Sunday — 271

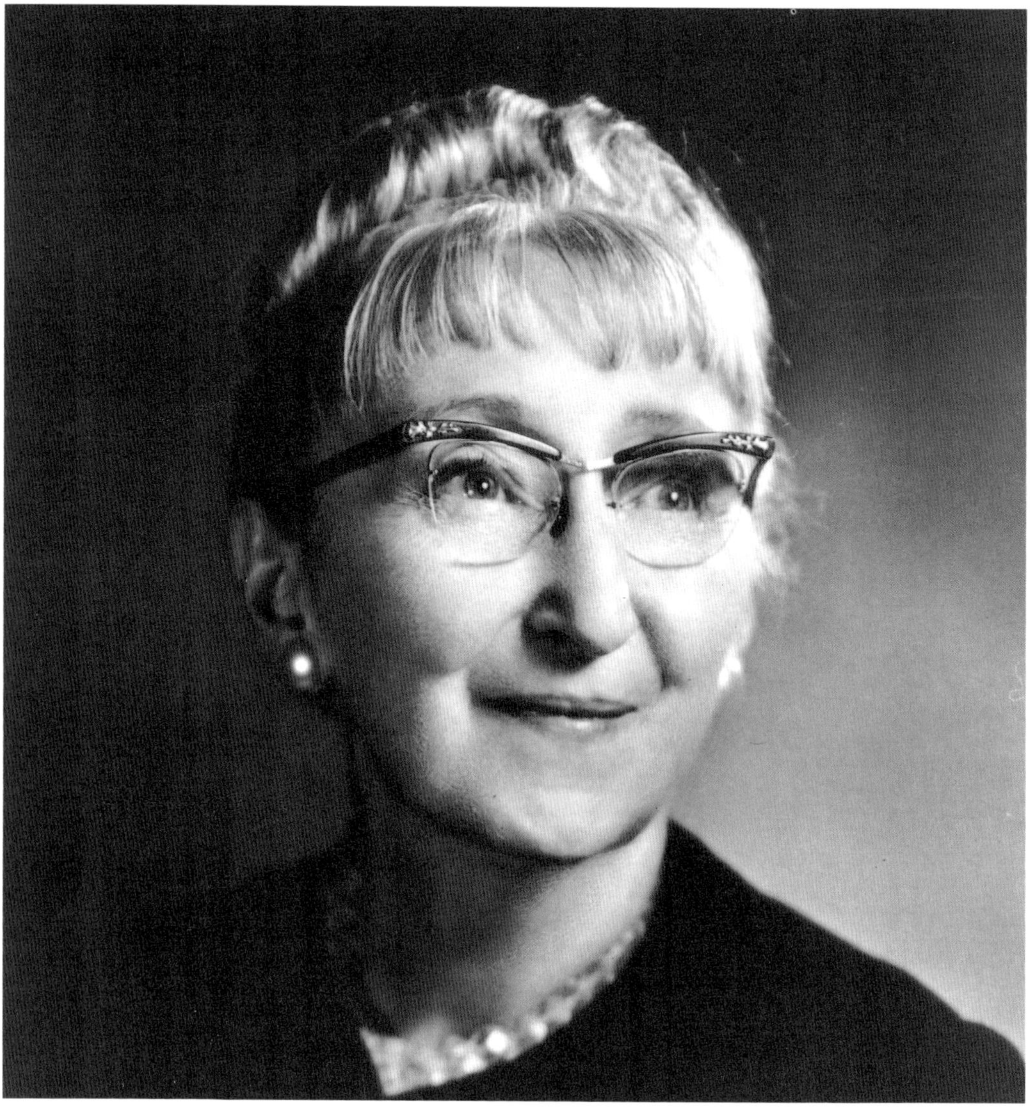

Sep/Oct

OCTOBER

S	M	T	W	T	F	S
			1	2	3	4
5	6	7	8	9	10	11
12	13	14	15	16	17	18
19	20	21	22	23	24	25
26	27	28	29	30	31	

SALLY CARRIGHAR
(1898–1985)
Naturalist, writer

A tiny mouse that was "singing" as it busily nested in Sally Carrighar's radio inspired her to leave her job as a radio show writer and combine her literary skills and longtime interest in animals to write about wildlife. "Within a month," she said, "I'd sold my first animal story." Born in Cleveland, Ohio, Carrighar overcame a troubled childhood to become an adventurer in diverse realms. From 1937 she made her living as a writer on wildlife and nature for general readers. The Walt Disney nature films *One Day at Beetle Rock* and *One Day at Teton Marsh,* which in the early 1950s introduced many a schoolchild to the beauty and diversity of North American flora and fauna, were based on Carrighar's first two books. She produced several others, and many first-person magazine pieces, on topics ranging from hunting with Eskimos to studying whales on the Channel Islands. An abiding respect for the rhythms of nature helped her get her stories. As she told a reporter, "If you sit in one place for a year or so, the animals come to you."

Society of Woman Geographers Collection
Manuscript Division

Congress passes Equal Credit Opportunity Act, 1974

29 Monday — 272

Sally Ride blasts off on six-day *Challenger* flight, 1983

30 Tuesday — 273

Entertainer Julie Andrews b. 1935

Rosh Hashanah (begins at sundown)
New Moon

1 Wednesday — 274

Designer Donna Karan b. 1948

2 Thursday — 275

Rebecca Felton becomes the first woman to occupy a seat in the U.S. Senate, 1922

3 Friday — 276

Bernice Johnson Reagon, historian, musician, and activist, b. 1942

4 Saturday — 277

Architect Maya Ying Lin, designer of Vietnam Veterans Memorial, b. 1959

5 Sunday — 278

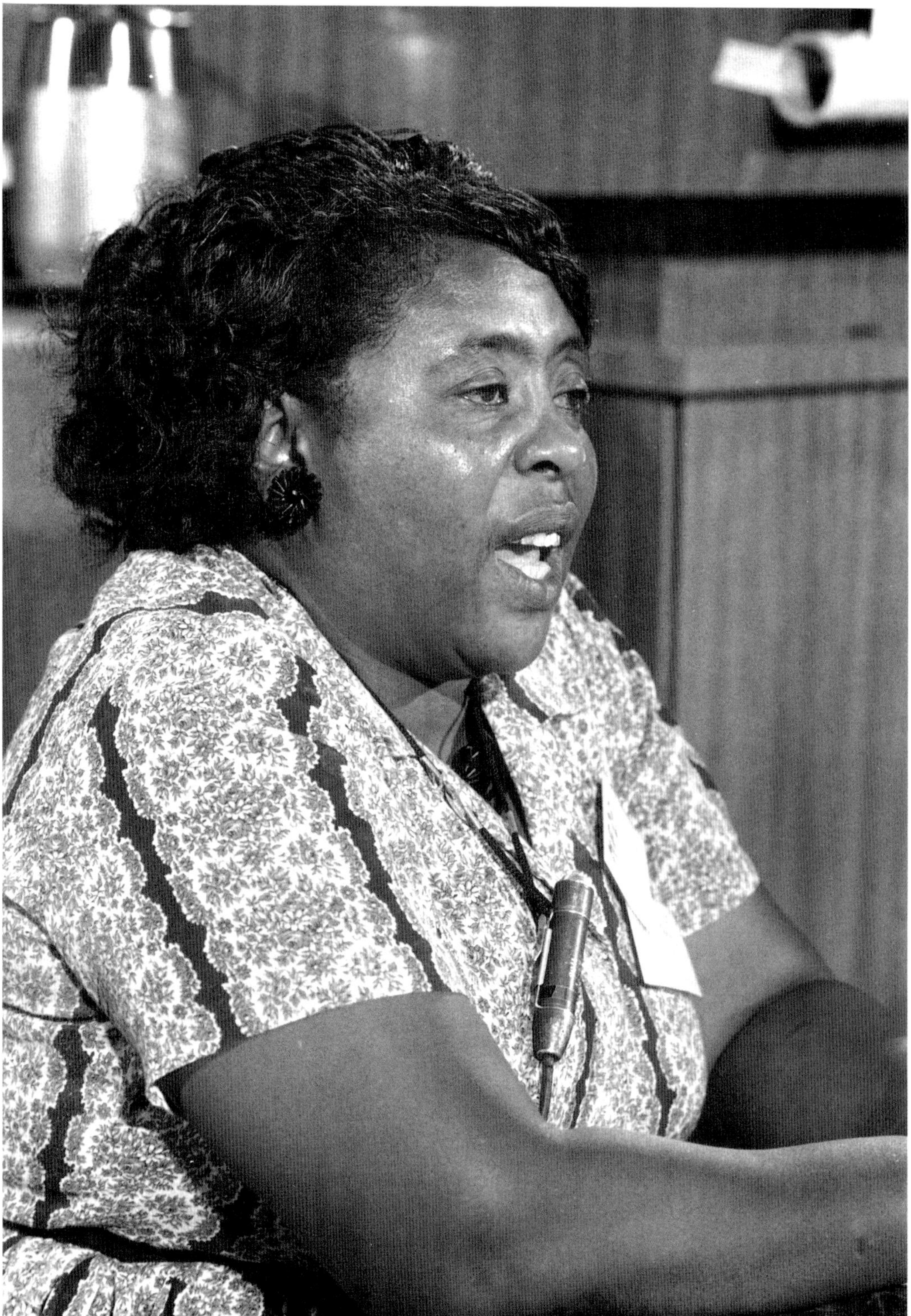

October

S	M	T	W	T	F	S
			1	2	3	4
5	6	7	8	9	10	11
12	13	14	15	16	17	18
19	20	21	22	23	24	25
26	27	28	29	30	31	

FANNIE LOU HAMER
(1917–1977)
Sharecropper, activist

Fannie Lou Hamer had worked for eighteen years as a sharecropper when, in 1962, her unsuccessful attempt to vote in her county seat of Indianola, Mississippi, brought severe economic reprisals and physical violence—and galvanized Hamer to civil rights activism for the rest of her life. Best known for her contributions to securing federally guaranteed voting rights for African Americans, Hamer was also a mover in economic and community development programs. As a founder of the Mississippi Freedom Democratic Party (MFDP), Hamer gained national attention during the 1964 Democratic National Convention, when the MFDP demanded to be seated along with the all-white regular state delegation. Hamer's dramatic leadership and oratory turned momentary defeat into an important media victory.

Beatings at the hands of police, which caused permanent damage to her arm and kidneys, never deterred Hamer. She embodied the ordinary African American's defiance of racial discrimination and terror—and the power that such defiance could unleash.

U.S. News and World Report Collection
Prints and Photographs Division

279
Fannie Lou Hamer, sharecropper and voting rights activist, b. 1917

6
Monday

280
Toni Morrison is awarded the Nobel Prize in literature, 1993

7
Tuesday

281
Actor Sigourney Weaver b. 1949

8
Wednesday

282
Naturalist and writer Sally Carrighar d. 1985

9
Thursday

First Quarter

283
Beatrice Hinkle, first female public health physician, b. 1874

10
Friday

Yom Kippur (begins at sundown)

284
Anita Hill testifies before the Senate Judiciary Committee regarding Supreme Court nominee Clarence Thomas, 1991

11
Saturday

285
Red Cross leader Mabel Boardman b. 1860

12
Sunday

Columbus Day

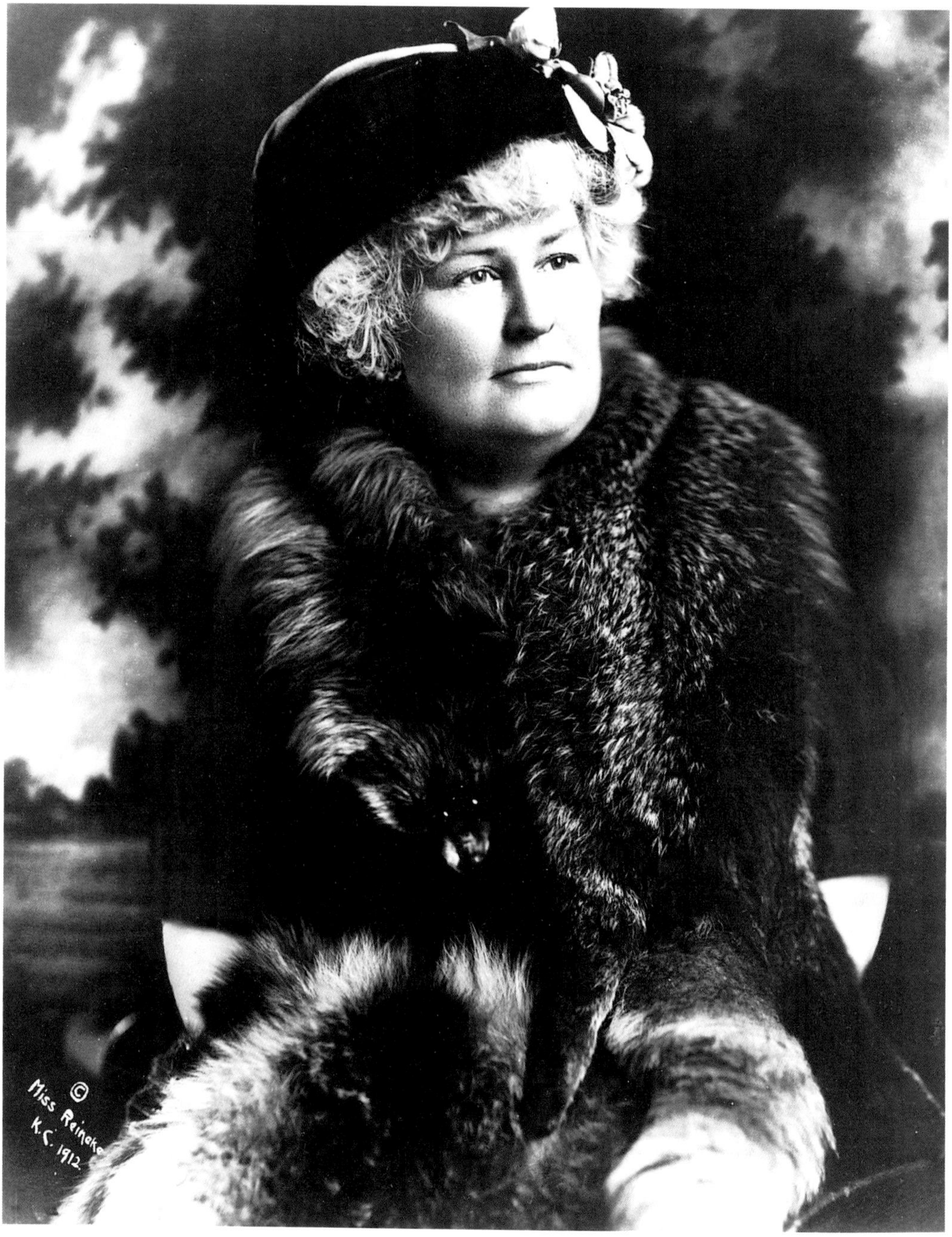
©
Miss Reineke
K.C. 1912

October

S	M	T	W	T	F	S
			1	2	3	4
5	6	7	8	9	10	11
12	13	14	15	16	17	18
19	20	21	22	23	24	25
26	27	28	29	30	31	

WINIFRED BLACK (ANNIE LAURIE)
(1863–1936)
Journalist

Fearless, innovative, and persistent, reporter Winifred Black, who wrote under the byline Annie Laurie, spared little effort in getting a story. To report about hospital conditions in San Francisco, she dressed as a beggar and pretended to faint in the middle of a street. Her resulting story of being thrown onto a prison cart and dragged to a substandard hospital led to hospital reform and the beginning of an ambulance service. To get an interview with President Benjamin Harrison, she hid under a table on the presidential train; to cover a tidal-wave disaster in Galveston, Texas, she dressed as a boy to get past police lines.

Black's unflinching reporting style and enterprising nature led her employer, William Randolph Hearst, to give her a variety of plum assignments—she covered nearly every important trial of her day, World War I, and the suffrage movement and was the first woman to cover a prizefight. Nevertheless, she considered herself "just a plain, practical all-around newspaperwoman. That is my profession and that is my pride."

Prints and Photographs Division

Pioneering African American jurist Edith Spurlock Sampson b. 1901

Columbus Day (Observed)
Thanksgiving Day (Canada)

13 Monday (286)

Intrepid journalist Winifred Black (Annie Laurie) b. 1863

14 Tuesday (287)

Scientist and birth control pioneer Marie Stopes b. 1880

15 Wednesday (288)

Margaret Sanger opens the first U.S. birth control clinic, New York City, 1916

Full Moon

16 Thursday (289)

Physician and astronaut Mae C. Jemison b. 1956

17 Friday (290)

Martina Navratilova, tennis great and gay rights spokeswoman, b. 1956

18 Saturday (291)

Mountaineer Annie Smith Peck b. 1850

19 Sunday (292)

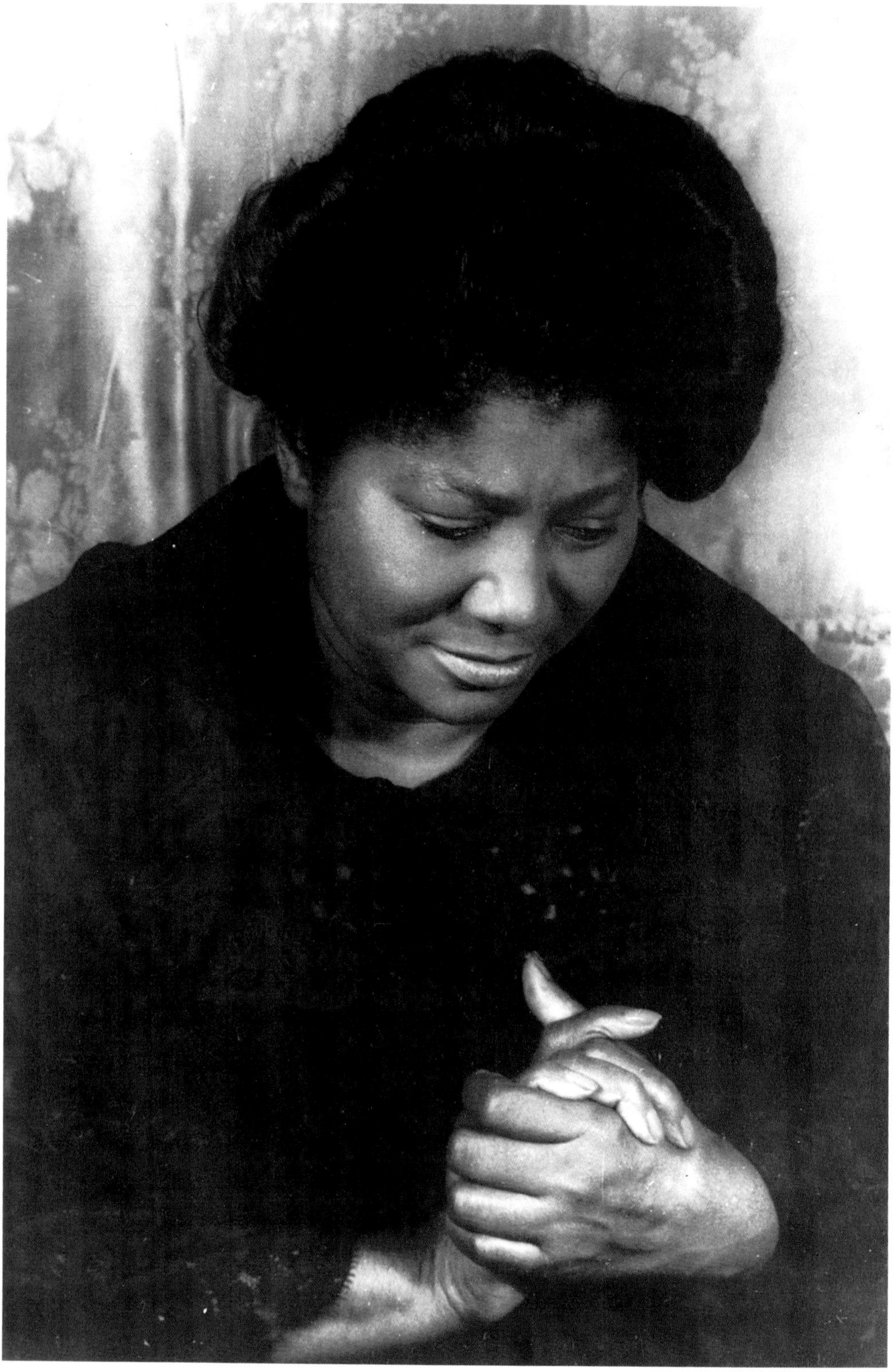

October

S	M	T	W	T	F	S
			1	2	3	4
5	6	7	8	9	10	11
12	13	14	15	16	17	18
19	20	21	22	23	24	25
26	27	28	29	30	31	

MAHALIA JACKSON
(1911–1972)
Gospel singer

A singer almost as soon as she could talk, Mahalia Jackson developed a powerful voice, driven by vibrant spiritual energy, that made her not only a living musical legend but a powerful force in the world. Raised in New Orleans, Jackson grew up under the dual influences of church music and the jazz/blues sounds of Jelly Roll Morton, King Oliver, and blues legend Bessie Smith. Moving to Chicago in 1928, she joined the choir of the Greater Salem Baptist Church and formed a gospel group as well. As word spread about her wondrous voice, invitations came from African American churches nationwide. She also stirred audiences at civil rights rallies throughout the 1950s and early 1960s—particularly with the music she made at the 1963 March on Washington before Martin Luther King's famous speech and at King's funeral. Jackson was a powerfully expressive, passionate singer—prompting some to criticize her "undignified" performances. Unfazed, she responded with her view that music was about much more than just sound: "I want my hands . . . my feet . . . my whole body to say all that is in me."
Prints and Photographs Division

Byllye Avery, founder of the Black Women's Health Network, b. 1937

20 Monday — 293

Grete Waitz becomes the first woman to run a marathon in under 2.5 hours, New York City, 1979

21 Tuesday — 294

Abigail Scott Duniway, Oregon journalist and lecturer on women's rights, b. 1834

22 Wednesday — 295

Long-distance swimmer Gertrude Ederle b. 1906

Last Quarter

23 Thursday — 296

Pioneering lawyer and U.S. presidential candidate Belva Lockwood b. 1830

United Nations Day

24 Friday — 297

Hanna Holborn Gray, president of the University of Chicago, b. 1930

25 Saturday — 298

Beryl Markham, aviator, adventurer, and author, b. 1902
Gospel legend Mahalia Jackson b. 1911

26 Sunday — 299

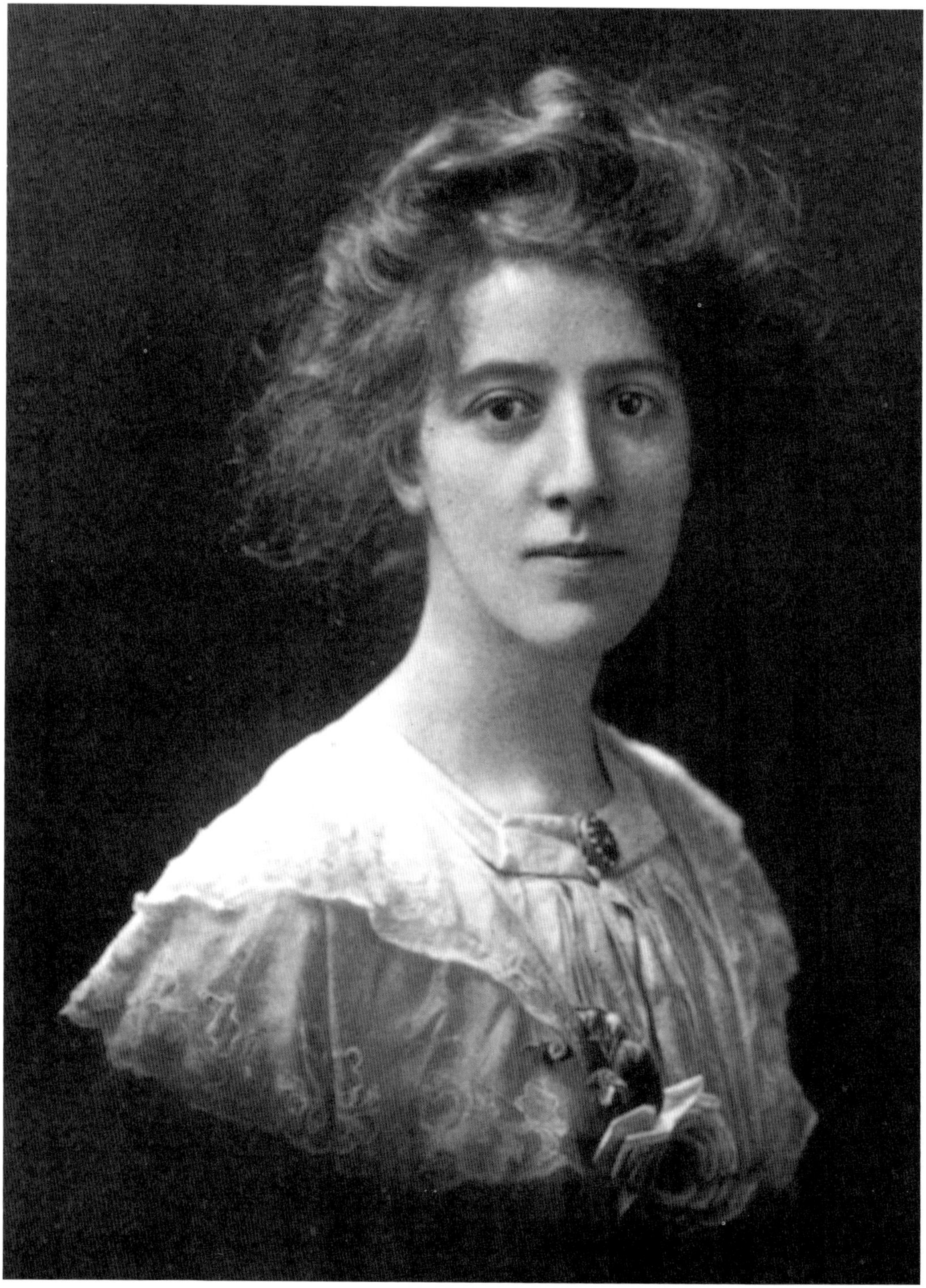

Oct/Nov

NOVEMBER
S	M	T	W	T	F	S
						1
2	3	4	5	6	7	8
9	10	11	12	13	14	15
16	17	18	19	20	21	22
23	24	25	26	27	28	29
30

MARIE STOPES
(1880–1958)
Scientist, birth control pioneer

When Marie Stopes and her second husband opened Britain's first birth control clinic in 1921, opposition from the medical and religious establishments was fierce. Typical was the rhetoric of one public-health official, who pronounced not only all contraception but also any public discussion thereof a "monstrous crime." Fortunately, Marie Stopes was anything but a shrinking violet. Daughter of a leisured scholar and a feminist pioneer of higher education, she was encouraged to pursue her interest in science, which led to a brilliant career as a paleobotanist and author. Problems in her first marriage, which was eventually annulled on grounds of nonconsummation, led her to read widely on sex and reproduction—and then to begin campaigning for greater public access to such information. Her 1916 book *Married Love* scandalized polite society—as much for its consideration of female pleasure as for its forthright treatment of sex in general—and was banned in the United States. Stopes devoted much of the rest of her life to the fight for birth control.

General Collections

Author Maxine Hong Kingston b. 1940

300
27
Monday

Suffragist and orator Anna Dickinson b. 1842

301
28
Tuesday

National Organization for Women (NOW) is founded, 1966

302
29
Wednesday

Gertrude Atherton, who pioneered the biographical novel form with *The Conqueror* (1902), b. 1857

303
30
Thursday

Singer and actor Ethel Waters b. 1900

Halloween
New Moon

304
31
Friday

Boston Female Medical School established, 1848

305
1
Saturday

Singer k. d. lang b. 1961

306
2
Sunday

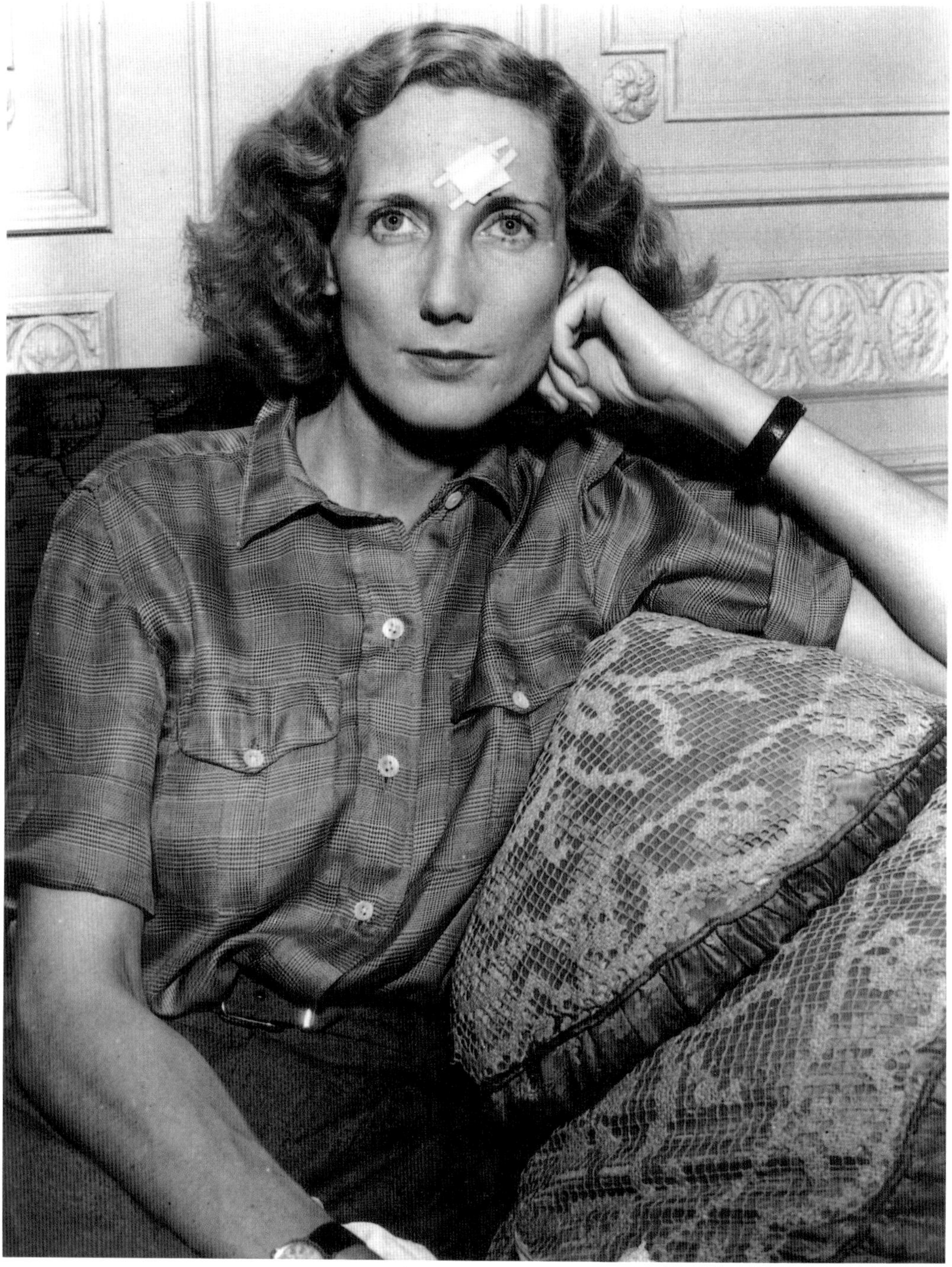

November

S	M	T	W	T	F	S
						1
2	3	4	5	6	7	8
9	10	11	12	13	14	15
16	17	18	19	20	21	22
23	24	25	26	27	28	29
30						

BERYL MARKHAM
(1902–1986)
Aviator, adventurer, horsewoman, author

One of the first women to receive a commercial pilot's license, Beryl Markham made history and international headlines when, in 1936, she became the first person to fly across the Atlantic from east to west. Born in England but raised by her father in Africa, Markham established her independence early, becoming a successful horse trainer and breeder and then a pilot. In 1942, she added writing to her list of accomplishments, publishing a volume of memoirs. *West with the Night* was praised by critics. ("Did you read Beryl Markham's book," Ernest Hemingway wrote to a friend. "[She] can write rings around us who consider ourselves writers.") Though Markham also wrote short stories, it is this poetic and atmospheric autobiography that best conveys not only the facts of her life but also its message: "I learned what every dreaming child needs to know—that no horizon is so far that you cannot get above it or beyond it."

New York World-Telegram and Sun Collection
Prints and Photographs Division

307
Comedian and television mogul Roseanne b. 1952

3
Monday

308
Carol Moseley-Braun becomes the first African American woman elected to the U.S. Senate, 1992

Election Day

4
Tuesday

309
Pioneering investigative journalist Ida Tarbell b. 1857

5
Wednesday

310
Tania Aebi completes a solo 27-month sailing voyage around the world, 1987

6
Thursday

311
Singer and songwriter Joni Mitchell b. 1943

First Quarter

7
Friday

312
Bonnie Raitt, first woman to have a signature model Fender Stratocaster electric guitar, b. 1949

8
Saturday

313
Poet Ann Sexton b. 1928

9
Sunday

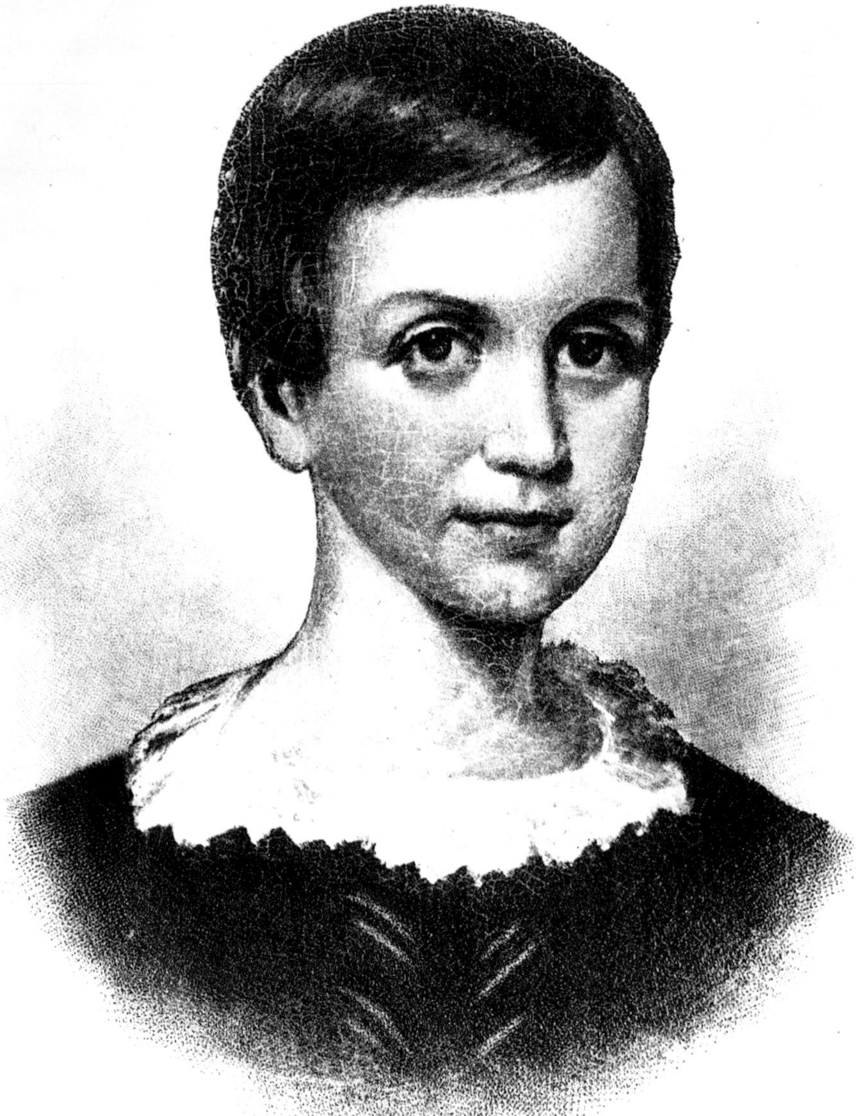

November

S	M	T	W	T	F	S
						1
2	3	4	5	6	7	8
9	10	11	12	13	14	15
16	17	18	19	20	21	22
23	24	25	26	27	28	29
30						

EMILY DICKINSON
(1830–1886)
Poet

Although she wrote more than 1,700 poems, Emily Dickinson (shown here in a youthful portrait from a book frontispiece) lived to see only seven of them in print. Her work, with its singular rhythms and unsentimental perspectives on love, death, and religion, challenged and confused the editors to whom she repeatedly submitted it. When it *was* published—both the handful of pieces published in her lifetime and those that appeared in posthumous collections—editors dulled and distorted her poems, inserting conventional punctuation and even substituting drab cliches for her incisive, bold words. In the twentieth century Dickinson's work, as originally penned, has gained her a place in the first rank of American letters. Though she lived as a physical recluse, Dickinson's art—including her beautiful, pithy correspondence—reveals a mind clearly unbounded by walls. When Daniel Chester French, a noted sculptor and acquaintance, received an honor, she wrote to him: "Success is dust, but an aim forever charged with dew. God keep you fundamental!"

Rare Book and Special Collections Division

Poet Emily Dickinson b. 1830

314
10
Monday

Abigail Adams b. 1744

Veterans Day
Remembrance Day (Canada)

315
11
Tuesday

Suffrage leader and freethinker Elizabeth Cady Stanton b. 1815

316
12
Wednesday

Comedian and actor Whoopi Goldberg b. 1955

317
13
Thursday

Claribel Cone, benefactor of the Baltimore Museum of Art, b. 1864

Full Moon

318
14
Friday

Painter Georgia O'Keeffe b. 1887

319
15
Saturday

Paula Giddings, author and historian of African American women, b. 1947

320
16
Sunday

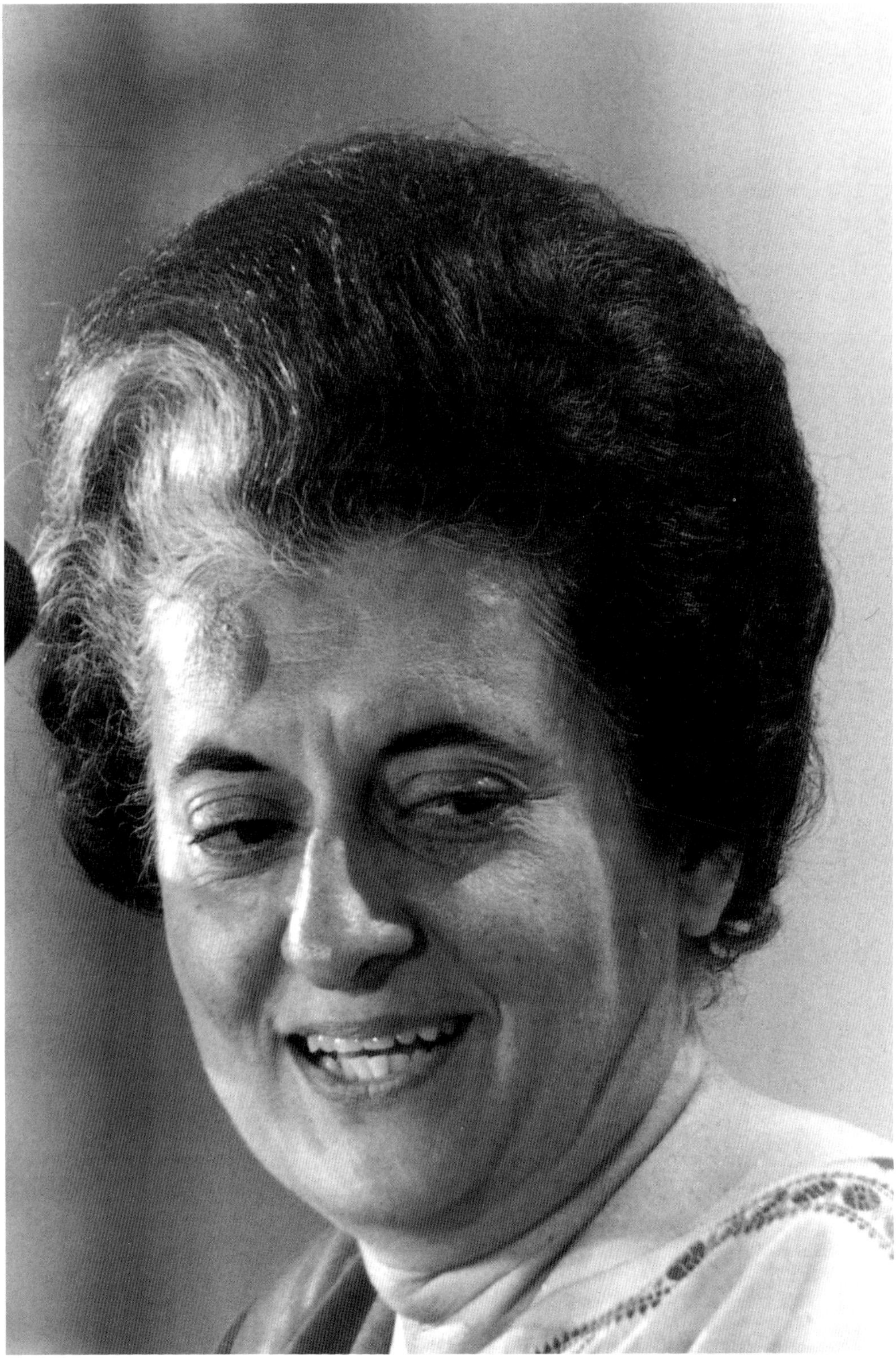

November

S	M	T	W	T	F	S
						1
2	3	4	5	6	7	8
9	10	11	12	13	14	15
16	17	18	19	20	21	22
23	24	25	26	27	28	29
30						

INDIRA GANDHI
(1917–1984)
Stateswoman

The only child of Jawaharlal and Kamala Nehru, who were both active (and often jailed) in the struggle for Indian independence, Indira Nehru grew up inspired by the spirit of Indian protest and its promise of social betterment. By age twelve she, too, was actively taking part, and by the time her widowed father took office as India's first prime minister in 1947, she was his political confidante and official hostess.

By the mid 1950s Indira Gandhi had become a prominent public figure in her own right. In 1959 she became president of the Indian National Congress, and in 1966, India's third prime minister. She served twice in that capacity; after being defeated in 1977, she was again elected in 1980. Although Gandhi was criticized for authoritarian rule, her legacy included major domestic reforms such as population control and a skillful balancing of East-West relations. Amidst rising factional violence, she was assassinated by Sikh extremists in 1984.

U.S. News and World Report Collection
Prints and Photographs Division

Religious leader Anne Hutchinson, convicted of "traducing the ministers," is banished from the Massachusetts Bay Colony, 1637

17 Monday — 321

Cherokee nation leader Wilma Mankiller b. 1945

18 Tuesday — 322

Indian stateswoman Indira Gandhi b. 1917

19 Wednesday — 323

Pauli Murray, lawyer, civil rights activist, and priest, b. 1910

20 Thursday — 324

Actor and feminist Marlo Thomas b. 1938

21 Friday — 325

Last Quarter

Billie Jean King, tennis great and women's sports advocate, b. 1943

22 Saturday — 326

Marie Van Vorst, author and reformer who exposed working conditions of women in factories, b. 1867

23 Sunday — 327

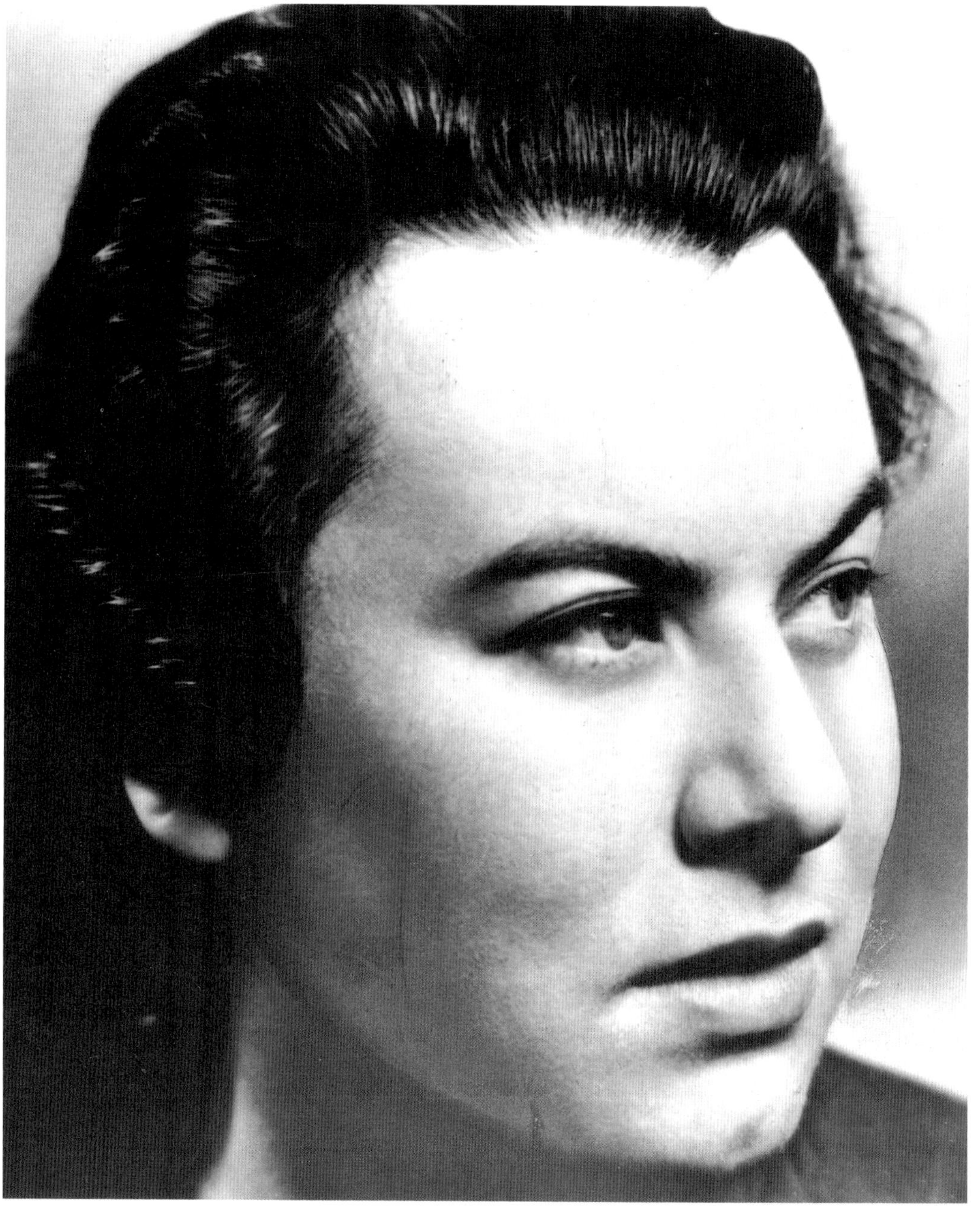

November

S	M	T	W	T	F	S
						1
2	3	4	5	6	7	8
9	10	11	12	13	14	15
16	17	18	19	20	21	22
23	24	25	26	27	28	29
30						

MURIEL RUKEYSER
(1913–1980)
Poet, author

"I am in the world / to change the world," wrote Muriel Rukeyser in a 1968 poem about artist Käthe Kollwitz. It was an apt summation of Rukeyser's own stance as a literary artist and social activist. Born in New York City, Rukeyser published her first poems while in college even as she was witnessing and reporting on such events as the racially explosive Scottsboro Boys trial. Eventually her wide-ranging intellect would produce, in addition to more than a dozen volumes of poetry, biographies of physicist Willard Gibbs and explorer Thomas Hariot; poetry translations from Swedish, French, German, and Italian; children's books; essays; television scripts; and a novel. But Rukeyser saw her mission as a poet—helping others to realize their fullest potentials of thought and feeling—as paramount. Near the end of her life, and in failing health, she traveled to South Korea to intervene on behalf of condemned poet Kim Chi-Ha. Not allowed to visit him, she held a vigil outside the prison gates; the experience yielded her last major poem, "The Gates."
New York World-Telegram and Sun Collection
Prints and Photographs Division

Nautical folk heroine Grace Darling b. 1815

24 Monday — 328

Temperance hell-raiser Carry Nation b. 1846

25 Tuesday — 329

Abolitionist and suffragist Sarah Grimke b. 1792

26 Wednesday — 330

Elsie Clews Parsons, pioneering anthropologist and teacher, b. 1875

Thanksgiving Day

27 Thursday — 331

Helen Magill White, educator and first U.S. woman to earn a Ph.D. degree (1877), b. 1853

28 Friday — 332

Nellie Tayloe Ross, first female U.S. governor (Wyoming, 1925–1927) and director of the Mint, b. 1876

29 Saturday — 333

Shirley Chisholm, first black U.S. congresswoman and presidential candidate, b. 1924

New Moon

30 Sunday — 334

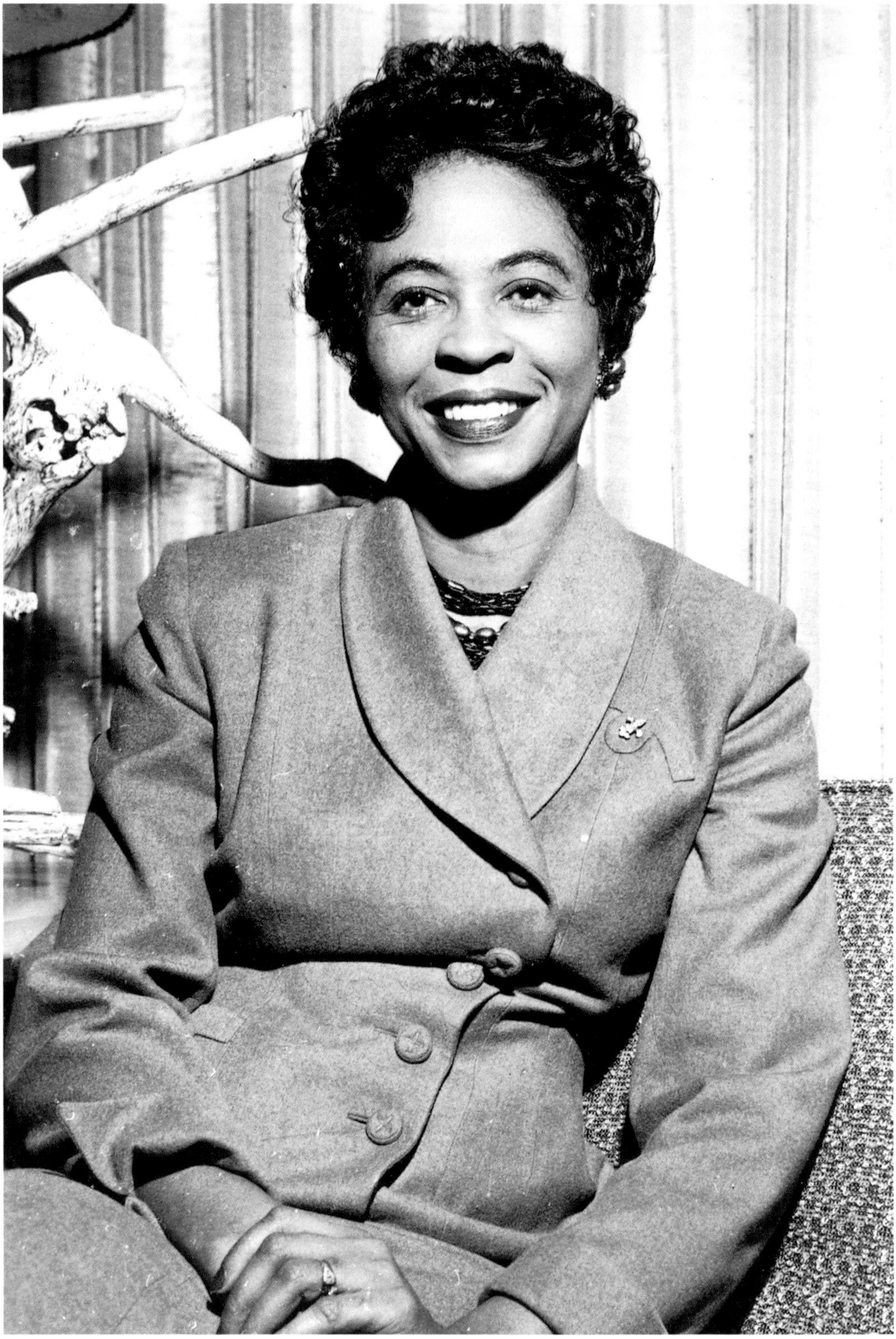

December

S	M	T	W	T	F	S
	1	2	3	4	5	6
7	8	9	10	11	12	13
14	15	16	17	18	19	20
21	22	23	24	25	26	27
28	29	30	31			

DAISY BATES
(b. 1914)
Activist, journalist

Civil rights leader Daisy Bates never knew her parents. Her mother had been abducted, assaulted, and murdered by three white men, and her father, grief-stricken and wary of reprisals if the murderers were prosecuted (they never were), fled the small town of Huttig, Arkansas, never to return. Bates, raised by adoptive parents, learned of the story at age eight; from it and her own experiences with racism grew a determination to do whatever she could to change a society that allowed such horrors to happen. As longtime co-editor (with her husband) of the *Arkansas State Press,* Bates used that newspaper to fight segregation, police brutality, and other injustices; and as president of the Arkansas NAACP, she organized the Little Rock Nine and engineered the desegregation of Little Rock's Central High School. Bates's leadership in that struggle was indomitable, even when her home was bombed and her newspaper became the target of economic reprisals. Honored as a pillar of the civil rights movement, Bates was also the only female pilot in the Arkansas Civil Air Patrol during World War II.

New York World-Telegram and Sun Collection
Prints and Photographs Division

Ann Preston, physician and founder of the Women's Hospital in Philadelphia, b. 1813

335
1
Monday

Tennis champion Monica Seles b. 1973

336
2
Tuesday

Opera legend Maria Callas b. 1923

337
3
Wednesday

Edith Cavell, nurse and patriot, b. 1865

338
4
Thursday

Elizabeth Agassiz, educator and first president of Radcliffe College, b. 1822

339
5
Friday

Patsy Mink, first Japanese American congresswoman and author of the Women's Educational Equity Act, b. 1927

340
6
Saturday

Multimedia artist Ellen Stewart b. 1919

341
7
Sunday

First Quarter

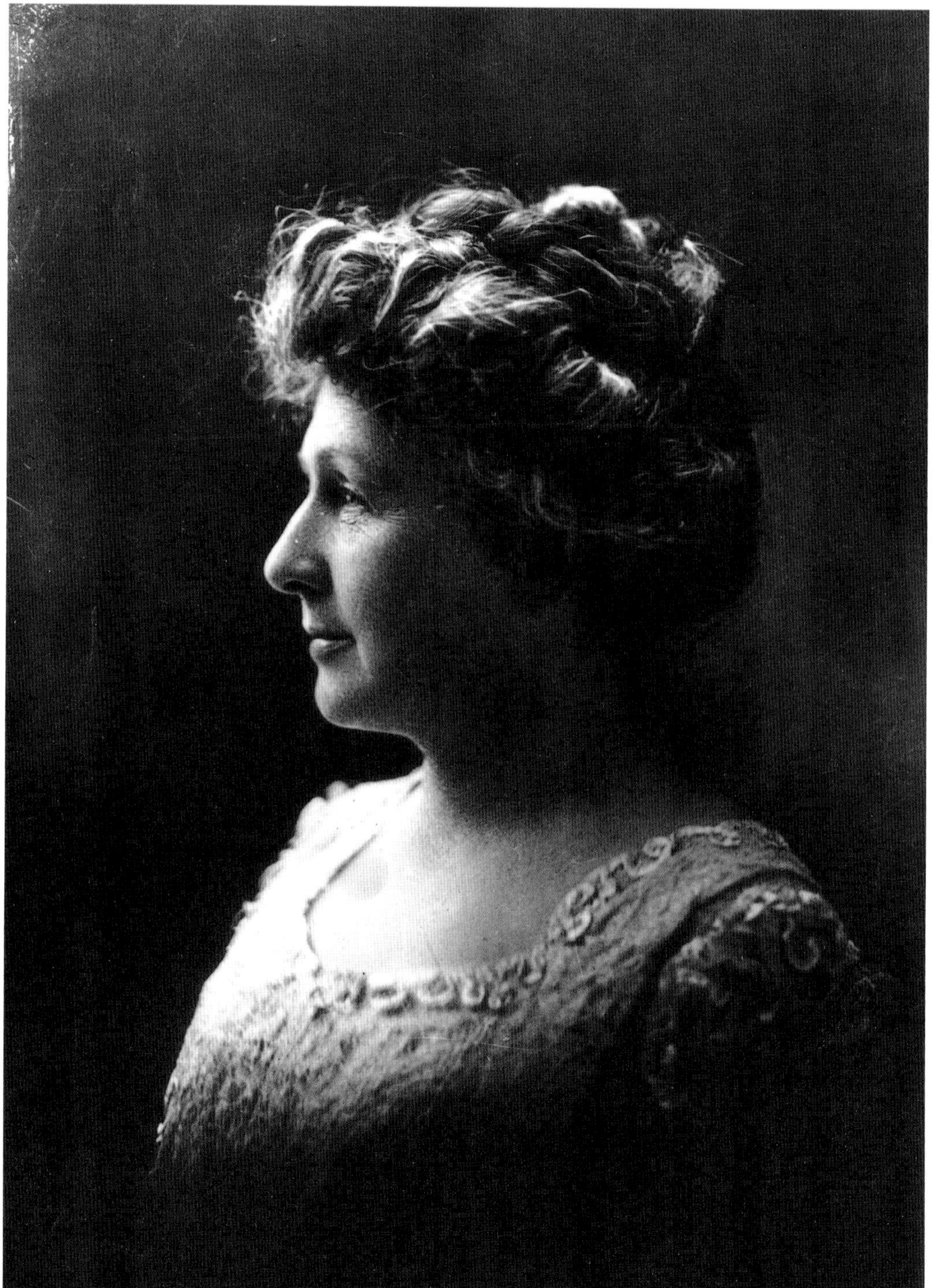

December

S	M	T	W	T	F	S
		1	2	3	4	5
						6
7	8	9	10	11	12	13
14	15	16	17	18	19	20
21	22	23	24	25	26	27
28	29	30	31			

ANNIE JUMP CANNON
(1863–1941)
Astronomer

Stargazer *par excellence,* Annie Jump Cannon marched from the halls of Wellesley and Radcliffe directly to the Harvard Observatory, where she made history in her field. She developed a stellar classification system that became Harvard's standard and went on to classify over 500,000 stars—more than any person had done—and oversee their cataloging and publication. It was one of the most significant achievements in twentieth-century astronomy and provided astrophysicists with a wealth of crucial new data for studying the evolution of the universe. During her long career, Cannon garnered many firsts and awards: she was the first person to systematically classify the heavens, the first woman to receive an honorary doctorate from Oxford University, and the first woman to be awarded the Draper Gold Medal of the National Academy of Sciences (though that male-dominated body never did elect her to membership). Cannon was also an honorary member of the Royal Astronomical Society and a member of the American Philosophical Society.

Prints and Photographs Division

Singer Sinead O'Connor b. 1966

8 Monday — 342

Computer language innovator Grace Hopper b. 1906

9 Tuesday — 343

Poet Emily Dickinson b. 1830

10 Wednesday — 344

Astronomer Annie Jump Cannon b. 1863

11 Thursday — 345

Toshiko Akiyoshi, jazz composer and bandleader, b. 1929

12 Friday — 346

Civil rights activist Ella Baker b. 1903

13 Saturday — 347

Senator and congresswoman Margaret Chase Smith b. 1897

14 Sunday — 348

Full Moon

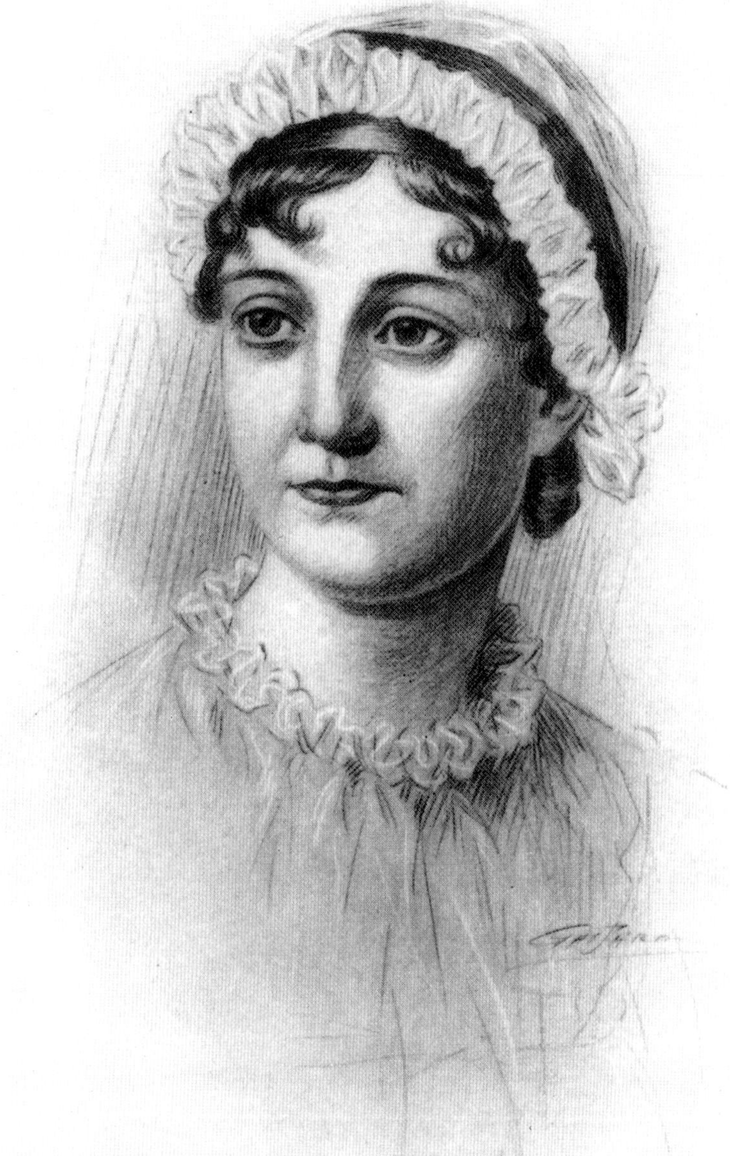

December

S	M	T	W	T	F	S
	1	2	3	4	5	6
7	8	9	10	11	12	13
14	15	16	17	18	19	20
21	22	23	24	25	26	27
28	29	30	31			

JANE AUSTEN
(1775–1817)
Writer

With stunning literary prowess, Jane Austen extracted timeless truths from the foibles and rituals of her largely homebound life. Raised in a lively and stimulating household in the Hampshire countryside, Austen first took up her pen as a girl, writing satirical pieces for her family's amusement. Gradually she honed her literary skills and developed an observational viewpoint at once sympathetic and ironic. With these she crafted the six novels of middle-class English domesticity that were pivotal in the development of the modern novel. Her first book, *Pride and Prejudice* (1796–1797), remains the most popular, though *Emma* and *Mansfield Park* (both 1811–1816) have been more admired by critics. Austen's portrayals of headstrong women, as in *Emma*, have a contemporary resonance that has fueled the Austen media boom of recent years (and spawned such awesome updates as the *Emma*-based *Clueless*). Though Austen lived only forty-two years, the reach of her art—now including a firm presence in cyberspace—seems only to grow with time.
General Collections

Poet and author Muriel Rukeyser b. 1913

15
Monday
349

Novelist Jane Austen b. 1775

16
Tuesday
350

Actor and singer Marlene Dietrich b. 1901

17
Wednesday
351

Gladys Henry Dick, microbiologist who isolated the bacterial cause of scarlet fever, b. 1881

18
Thursday
352

Actor Cicely Tyson b. 1933

19
Friday
353

Ethel Barrymore Theater opens in New York City, 1928

20
Saturday
354

Rebecca West, author, critic, and feminist, b. 1892

Winter Solstice 8:07 P.M. (GMT)
Last Quarter

21
Sunday
355

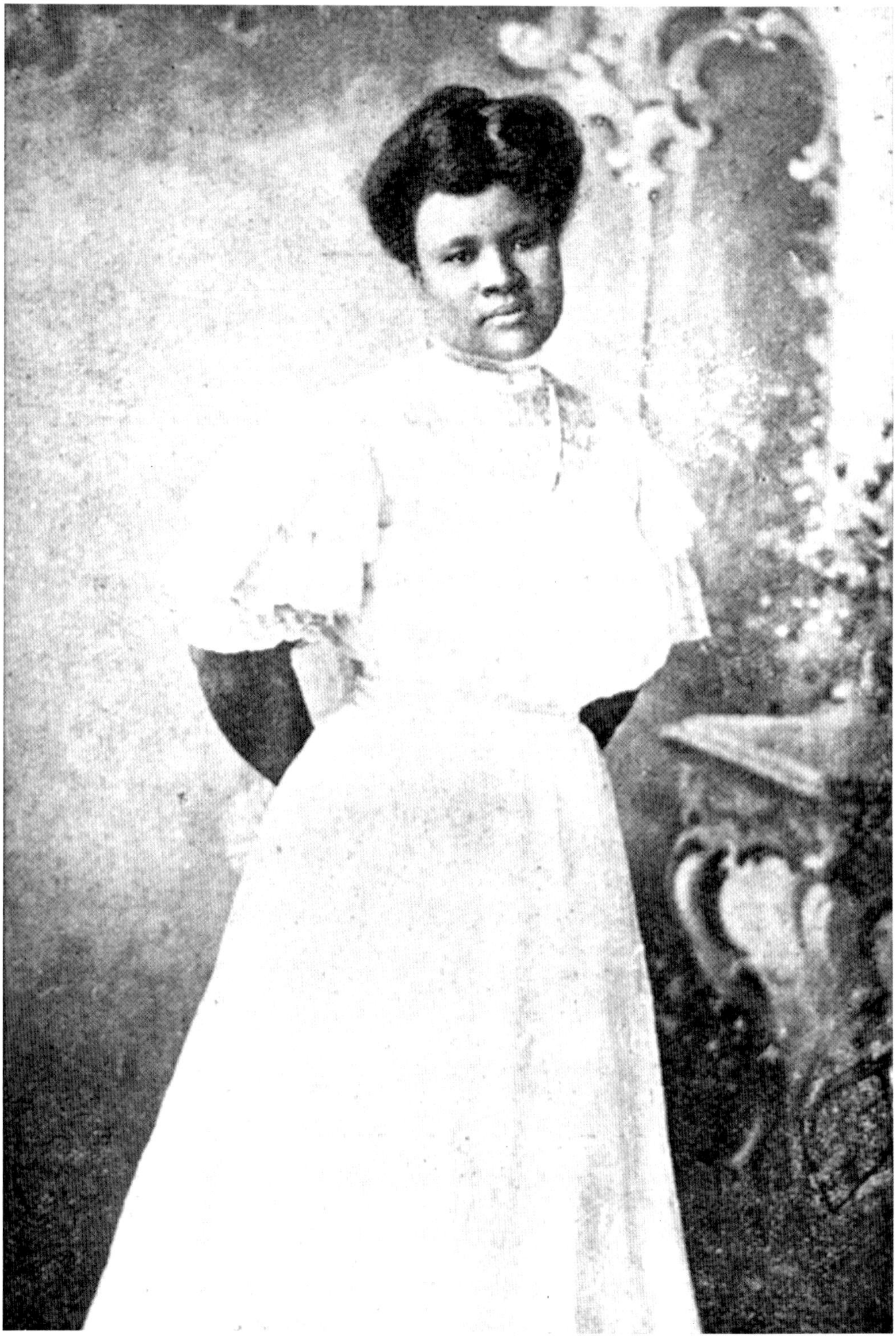

December

S	M	T	W	T	F	S
		1	2	3	4	5	6
7	8	9	10	11	12	13
14	15	16	17	18	19	20
21	22	23	24	25	26	27
28	29	30	31			

MADAME C. J. WALKER
(1867–1919)
Entrepreneur

Born in Delta, Louisiana, raised on farms there and in Mississippi, married by age fourteen, and widowed at twenty, Madame C. J. Walker (born Sarah Breedlove) went on to become a successful hair and cosmetics entrepreneur—and, by the early twentieth century, the richest self-made woman in America. But Walker saw her personal wealth not as an end in itself but as a means to help promote and expand economic opportunities for others, especially African Americans. She took great pride in the profitable employment—and alternative to domestic labor—that her company afforded many thousands of black women who worked as commissioned agents. Walker was also well known for her philanthropy, supporting African American educational and social institutions from the national to the grass roots levels. Walker's daughter, A'Leila, carried on this tradition, opening her mother's home and her own to writers and artists of the emergent Harlem Renaissance and becoming a catalytic figure in that movement.

Manuscript Division

Theatrical designer Aline Bernstein b. 1880

356
22
Monday

Mme. C. J. Walker (Sarah Breedlove), self-made cosmetics magnate and philanthropist, b. 1867

Hanukkah (begins at sundown)

357
23
Tuesday

Elizabeth Chandler, abolitionist author who supported boycotting of goods made by slave labor, b. 1807

358
24
Wednesday

Singer Annie Lennox b. 1954

Christmas Day

359
25
Thursday

Sled-dog racing champion Susan Butcher b. 1954

Boxing Day (Canada)
New Moon

360
26
Friday

Newswoman and commentator Cokie Roberts b. 1943

361
27
Saturday

Elizabeth Lucas Pinckney, plantation manager who introduced indigo into South Carolina, b. 1722

362
28
Sunday

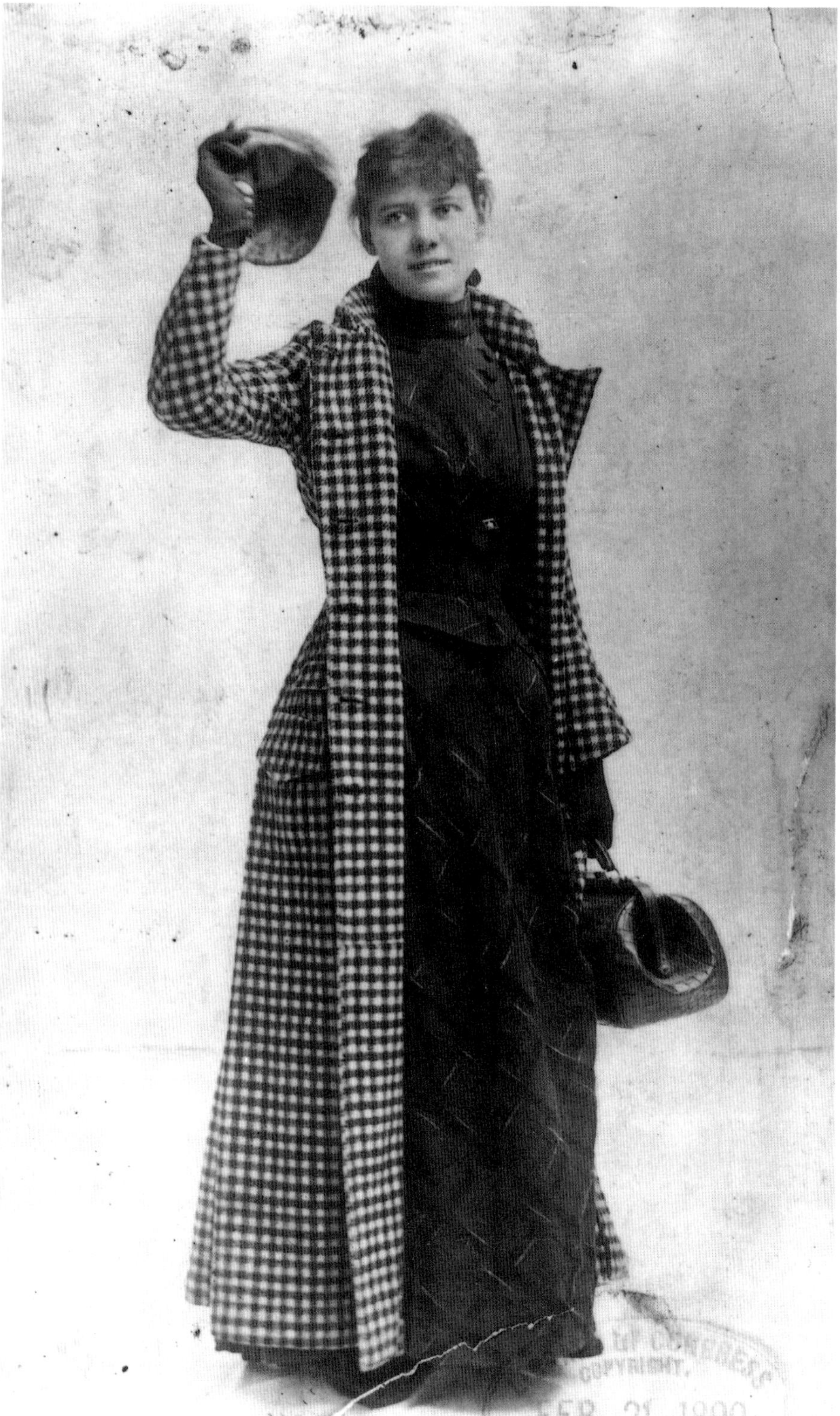
COPYRIGHT.
FEB 21 1890

Dec/Jan

JANUARY
S	M	T	W	T	F	S
				1	2	3
4	5	6	7	8	9	10
11	12	13	14	15	16	17
18	19	20	21	22	23	24
25	26	27	28	29	30	31

NELLIE BLY (ELIZABETH COCHRANE)
(1867–1922)
Journalist

Elizabeth Cochrane, who took her pen name of Nellie Bly from a popular Stephen Foster song, was the best-known "girl reporter" of her day, not only for her colorful exploits—most notably a 1888–1889 solo round-the-world voyage in seventy-two days—but also for her skill and resourcefulness as an investigative journalist. Largely self-educated, Bly embarked on her reporting career in her early twenties, quickly taking on such volatile subjects as political corruption and problems of working women. To gain employment at the *New York World* in 1887, Bly finagled admission as a patient to Blackwell's Island, a notorious mental institution; her articles exposing its inhumane conditions led to a grand jury investigation and several million dollars' worth of improvements.

Similar journalistic exploits revealed abominable conditions in sweatshops, jails, and other institutions—not to mention bribery in the New York legislature. After her death, the *Evening Journal* eulogized her as having been "the best reporter in America."

Prints and Photographs Division

Physician and surgeon Rosa Gantt b. 1875

29 Monday — 363

Rachel Foster Avery, suffragist and assistant to Susan B. Anthony, b. 1858

30 Tuesday — 364

Singer and songwriter Odetta b. 1930

31 Wednesday — 365

Betsy Ross b. 1752

New Year's Day, 1998

1 Thursday — 1

M. Carey Thomas, pioneer of women's higher education, b. 1857

2 Friday — 2

Lucretia Coffin Mott, abolitionist and women's rights leader, b. 1793

3 Saturday — 3

Selena Butler, advocate-leader of interracial cooperation, b. 1872

4 Sunday — 4

1997

JANUARY

S	M	T	W	T	F	S
			1	2	3	4
5	6	7	8	9	10	11
12	13	14	15	16	17	18
19	20	21	22	23	24	25
26	27	28	29	30	31	

MAY

S	M	T	W	T	F	S
				1	2	3
4	5	6	7	8	9	10
11	12	13	14	15	16	17
18	19	20	21	22	23	24
25	26	27	28	29	30	31

SEPTEMBER

S	M	T	W	T	F	S
	1	2	3	4	5	6
7	8	9	10	11	12	13
14	15	16	17	18	19	20
21	22	23	24	25	26	27
28	29	30				

FEBRUARY

S	M	T	W	T	F	S
						1
2	3	4	5	6	7	8
9	10	11	12	13	14	15
16	17	18	19	20	21	22
23	24	25	26	27	28	

JUNE

S	M	T	W	T	F	S
1	2	3	4	5	6	7
8	9	10	11	12	13	14
15	16	17	18	19	20	21
22	23	24	25	26	27	28
29	30					

OCTOBER

S	M	T	W	T	F	S
			1	2	3	4
5	6	7	8	9	10	11
12	13	14	15	16	17	18
19	20	21	22	23	24	25
26	27	28	29	30	31	

MARCH

S	M	T	W	T	F	S
						1
2	3	4	5	6	7	8
9	10	11	12	13	14	15
16	17	18	19	20	21	22
23	24	25	26	27	28	29
30	31					

JULY

S	M	T	W	T	F	S
		1	2	3	4	5
6	7	8	9	10	11	12
13	14	15	16	17	18	19
20	21	22	23	24	25	26
27	28	29	30	31		

NOVEMBER

S	M	T	W	T	F	S
						1
2	3	4	5	6	7	8
9	10	11	12	13	14	15
16	17	18	19	20	21	22
23	24	25	26	27	28	29
30						

APRIL

S	M	T	W	T	F	S
		1	2	3	4	5
6	7	8	9	10	11	12
13	14	15	16	17	18	19
20	21	22	23	24	25	26
27	28	29	30			

AUGUST

S	M	T	W	T	F	S
					1	2
3	4	5	6	7	8	9
10	11	12	13	14	15	16
17	18	19	20	21	22	23
24	25	26	27	28	29	30
31						

DECEMBER

S	M	T	W	T	F	S
	1	2	3	4	5	6
7	8	9	10	11	12	13
14	15	16	17	18	19	20
21	22	23	24	25	26	27
28	29	30	31			

1998

JANUARY

S	M	T	W	T	F	S
				1	2	3
4	5	6	7	8	9	10
11	12	13	14	15	16	17
18	19	20	21	22	23	24
25	26	27	28	29	30	31

FEBRUARY

S	M	T	W	T	F	S
1	2	3	4	5	6	7
8	9	10	11	12	13	14
15	16	17	18	19	20	21
22	23	24	25	26	27	28

MARCH

S	M	T	W	T	F	S
1	2	3	4	5	6	7
8	9	10	11	12	13	14
15	16	17	18	19	20	21
22	23	24	25	26	27	28
29	30	31				

APRIL

S	M	T	W	T	F	S
			1	2	3	4
5	6	7	8	9	10	11
12	13	14	15	16	17	18
19	20	21	22	23	24	25
26	27	28	29	30		

MAY

S	M	T	W	T	F	S
					1	2
3	4	5	6	7	8	9
10	11	12	13	14	15	16
17	18	19	20	21	22	23
24	25	26	27	28	29	30
31						

JUNE

S	M	T	W	T	F	S
	1	2	3	4	5	6
7	8	9	10	11	12	13
14	15	16	17	18	19	20
21	22	23	24	25	26	27
28	29	30				

JULY

S	M	T	W	T	F	S
			1	2	3	4
5	6	7	8	9	10	11
12	13	14	15	16	17	18
19	20	21	22	23	24	25
26	27	28	29	30	31	

AUGUST

S	M	T	W	T	F	S
						1
2	3	4	5	6	7	8
9	10	11	12	13	14	15
16	17	18	19	20	21	22
23	24	25	26	27	28	29
30	31					

SEPTEMBER

S	M	T	W	T	F	S
		1	2	3	4	5
6	7	8	9	10	11	12
13	14	15	16	17	18	19
20	21	22	23	24	25	26
27	28	29	30			

OCTOBER

S	M	T	W	T	F	S
				1	2	3
4	5	6	7	8	9	10
11	12	13	14	15	16	17
18	19	20	21	22	23	24
25	26	27	28	29	30	31

NOVEMBER

S	M	T	W	T	F	S
1	2	3	4	5	6	7
8	9	10	11	12	13	14
15	16	17	18	19	20	21
22	23	24	25	26	27	28
29	30					

DECEMBER

S	M	T	W	T	F	S
		1	2	3	4	5
6	7	8	9	10	11	12
13	14	15	16	17	18	19
20	21	22	23	24	25	26
27	28	29	30	31		

Notes